D0048892

The Skipping Stone

The Skipping Stone

Ripple Effects of Mental Illness on the Family

by Mona Wasow

Science and Behavior Books, Inc.
PALO ALTO, CALIFORNIA

SBB

Copyright © 1995 by Science & Behavior Books, Inc. All rights reserved. No part of this book may be reproduced without permission from the publisher.

Printed in the United States of America.

Library of Congress Card Number 94-069598

ISBN 0-8314-0082-X

Cover design by Gary LaRochelle/Flea Ranch Graphics
Editing and interior design by Rain Blockley
Typesetting by Robin Penninger
Printing by Haddon Craftsmen

Royalties on this book are donated by the author to the National Alliance for the Mentally Ill.

To
David Jonathan Murie
who has taught me about courage

CONTENTS

PREFACE

This is exactly how it happened. The idea for a book was already there, and three chapters had been written. I looked them over one night and thought: "This is awful. One chapter reads as if it were meant for clinicians, another for family members, and still another for educators. What am I doing?" I went to bed in a foul mood and woke up at 3 a.m. with a start: "One Voice!"

Now, what does that mean? Should I ponder this or have a salami sandwich?

I thought about it. I even paid attention to the sadness I was feeling. The sadness had to do with the endless misunderstandings between and within groups of people, all of whom care deeply about the plight of mentally ill people. Then the importance hit me of all these different perspectives and components: what people with mental illness thought and felt, what family members had to say, what clinicians were doing and believing, what the researchers were finding, and what teachers were teaching. It seemed vital to bridge the gap and find one voice for all. This book is my humble attempt.

So that is what the rude awakening was all about. Then I had the salami sandwich and restarted this book. Strange happenings in the middle of the night.

ACKNOWLEDGMENTS

First and foremost, I want to thank the people who so willingly shared their stories and feelings with my researchers and me. Without them there would be no book. I am grateful to all the wonderful social work students who did most of the interviewing with sensitivity and compassion, and with the ability to learn from the experience.

I thank Rain Blockley for her careful, talented editing and good cheer, and Bob Slpitzer of Science and Behavior Books for his faith and willingness to take me on board again.

Debra Komro and Donna Murdoch are not only excellent typists, but they are knowledgeable about the topic and good friends, to boot.

Friends and colleagues looked over various chapters and gave both wise counsel and encouraging words: Anne Deveson, Sue Estroff, Carol Grogan, Tom Hickey, Harriet Lefly, Helen Schneyer, Mildred M. Seltzer, and Mary Ann Test. Special thanks to Kate Judge and Sue Estroff for their helpful review of chapter 2; and to Beth Angel, David Delap, Stephanie Guth, Voyce Hendrix, Mary Hoefler, Kate Judge, Kevin Kiefaber, Jeanette Lytle, Janet Pederson, and Anne Tellett for their compassionate interviewing. Thanks also to Dzidra Anderson, who collected some of the data for chapter 11 from the Clinton-Eaton-Ingham Community Mental Health Center in Lansing, Michigan.

Special love to Oliver Wasow and Robin Murie, who bravely and lovingly travel this journey with me. Thanks to Wolfgang,

Bernard, and Tommy Wasow, who remain steadfast toward David throughout. And to my close friends and family who sustain me; to my dedicated fellow NAMI members; and to my colleagues at the University of Wisconsin School of Social Work. I also feel indebted to the inspiring, caring students in the severe-mental-illness field unit, with whom I have had the privilege of turning this journey of pain into one of purpose and meaning.
      I thank you all so much.

Mona Wasow
Plainfield, Vermont
July 1994

I

A LONELY JOURNEY:

Mental Illness in the Family

There once was a big place in our hearts for my son, filled with his laughter, brightness, and mischief. Now he stands mute, eyes of pain asking if we have abandoned him. We haven't really, but he seems like a bottomless pit that remains empty no matter how much love we pour into him. And we are left drained.

Did any of us see it coming? When did he first start changing? He used to be great, then he was not; but surely it would pass. If he could just make some friends again; maybe a different school; maybe music lessons; or more attention ... or less attention. But he just got worse and worse. We kept trying to fix things. The quarrels, scenes, failures, and screaming continued, no matter what we did. Our love could not stop the inevitable push toward insanity. Now, twenty years later, it is even worse in some ways: a quiet withdrawal into nothingness, a sadness with no end.

"So much of my childhood was lost to his illness," says his younger brother.

"If you had stayed home and not worked, it would not have happened," accuses the heartbroken, confused grandmother.

"What did we do wrong?" his father and I ask.

Other relatives argue about whether it was bad genes or bad environment, and they remain loyal. One second cousin assures me that he will look after my son after I die. Another distant relative has never even seen my son but lives under the shadow of fear that the hidden illness will somehow attack him, or his children.

On and on it goes. Like dervish devils we twist and turn, argue and cry. Then we give up for awhile, quiet down, stop talking to each other about it until it all starts up again. Will it never end? No—unless maybe he dies. But then previous conversations come to mind with other people whose mentally ill relatives had died. They were still agonizing. So if there is no end, then what? This book tries to redirect some of the pain into constructive channels.

For the past twenty years, my involvement in the mental illness arena has been inextricably woven together while wearing three hats: first and foremost, the hat of an endlessly grieving mother; second, that of a social work educator; and third, that of a clinician. Twenty years ago I was primarily concerned with family members because we had been desperately neglected by professionals, at best. At worst, we were blamed. Now, with advances in our knowledge about severe mental illnesses (SMI), the picture is changing for the better. Some wonderful, compassionate professionals are on the horizon. Increasingly the distinctions among my three hats are blurring, and in this spirit, I find myself wanting to reach families, educators, and clinicians alike. We all have a common enemy: SMI. SMI in this book refers to the affective disorders and the schizophrenias. Other SMIs exist but were not included in our study.

I attempt to wear all three hats as I write, in hopes that the three groups will benefit from seeing each other's different perspectives. It is probably unrealistic to hope for agreement on many of the volatile issues that surround SMI. Because so many unknowns remain about these devastating illnesses and the best ways of treating them, there are bound to be many areas of disagreement. The less people know, the greater their insecurities and, in turn, the more vociferous their disagreements. The end result is that energy drains away from our common goal of alleviating as much suffering as possible for all concerned.

We may not be able to convince one another about topics such as the need for more protection versus deinstitutionalization, voluntary versus involuntary medications, the use of electric shock therapy, and so on. It would help, however, if we could at least get some idea of where other people are coming from, and why. The ability to stand in the shoes of another is a splendid one. It can reduce friction—something presently needed among family members, professionals (including educators, clinicians, and researchers), and people with severe mental illnesses.

This book reviews some of the literature on family stress, reports experiences obtained by interviewing extended family members, and suggests clinical implications for practice. The end results may be as awkward as wearing three hats, but the intention is to find one voice for all. And with that one voice, may we show mercy toward all—because this is a lonely journey, and we need each other.

The Ripple Effect

As with a large stone skipping across water, the ripple effect of mental illness on the entire family is enormous. This is not surprising, given the severity of mental illnesses, the prejudice toward people who have them, the ignorance about them in our culture, and the fears most family members have about the genetic basis of such illnesses. In addition, it is our brains that make us distinctly human. When someone's brain malfunctions, contrasted with any other bodily breakdown, we find it more difficult to know and see the human being within.

The past ten to fifteen years have seen researchers beginning to write about families of the mentally ill. It is a good beginning. After many years of talking with families, teaching, and doing workshops in this area, I have become increasingly aware of SMI's enormous impact on the extended family as well as the immediate family. Most of the family literature, however, confines itself to the experiences of parents—probably the minority of parents, at that.

Some literature exists on siblings, less on spouses and children of mentally ill parents, and nothing on grandparents or extended family members such as aunts, uncles, cousins, nieces, or nephews. The literature's other big omission is parents who, for whatever reasons, have very little or no contact with their mentally ill adult children. What has happened to these parents? Why have they dropped away? This very complex topic will not be handled in this book, but it is essential to point out that we are missing information about an imporant group of family members. If we understood how and why these parents were dropping away, we might find ways of being more helpful to all concerned.

Our Study

.   This book attempts a portrait of the immediate family as well as other relatives who may not have lived in the same household with the SMI member. To this end, a few well-trained social work students and I interviewed one hundred people. We did in-depth interviews with twenty people from each of the above-mentioned categories. In addition to what these people told us about their experiences, our palette included a literature review in each category, exploring what professionals (researchers and clinicians) and family members had to say. (Interview guidelines and letter are in the apendices.)

Also included in this portrait are a few additional areas surrounding the phenomenon of having mental illness in the family. One of these is the grief process. Most relatives reported a sadness without resolution or end. Closely tied to this is the process of coping, which also appears to be ever changing and never ending.

Hope, and sometimes lack of hope, seems very significant in how people cope. This led us to look at some of the differences among relatives, professionals, and mentally ill people regarding their perspectives on hope. We tried to find out what hopes they held for themselves, their children, or their clients.

Another issue, hard to capture in words, comes under the heading of "To Say It Out Loud Just Once." Living with mental illness in the family is extremely stressful, and people are sometimes driven to desperate thoughts and feelings. Because our culture

frowns on the expression of miserable, bleak, or negative thoughts about family, most people tend to keep such thoughts and feelings to themselves. This causes no end of grief as they boomerang into guilt and remorse. There may be no way of eliminating the sadness over seeing a loved one suffer, or the feelings of loss for oneself, but perhaps some of the destructive power of these thoughts can be reduced by saying them out loud and acknowledging their existence. Thoughts are free, after all, and they do not kill. They just are.

Many relatives have expressed these negative feelings to each other but feel they are too terrible to express to anyone else. I think professionals need to hear them, and some family members will feel relieved to know they are not the only ones to have such desperate thoughts. We need to expand the parameters of what are considered "normal" thoughts and feelings.

LIMITATIONS

These data by no means tell us about all extended family members. They have certain limitations. Our sample came only from the midwestern United States and was largely white and middle class. This does not tell us about the experiences of people from other parts of the world or other parts of this country. Nor does it capture any vast cultural, economic, ethnic, or individual differences. Our sample was voluntary, so we do not know about people who do not wish to be interviewed.

Another factor that confounds our findings is that various volunteers' relatives had been ill over a wide range of time: from one to forty-five years. (The advantage, of course, was that this gave us a window on process.) Nor did our interviews separate the schizophrenias from the affective disorders, and it is certainly possible that different illnesses have different effects on extended family members.

Our research was cross-sectional rather than longitudinal, which has the limitation of examining a person's experience and memory at only one stage. People do change their perspectives over time. In studying a group as diverse and complex as extended family members of mentally ill people, we can never assume that one person, or a hundred people, speak for all. Our sample is biased by having interviewed family members who have very ill relatives. We know this is not the whole picture, because some mentally ill people get considerably better.

It is necessary to acknowledge a huge number of contingencies. The adjustments and coping capacities of the affluent may be different from those of the very poor, for instance, and variations occur because of gender, age, relationship to the relative, ethnicity, religion, and just plain individual differences. It is clear that, to draw a broad profile of extended family members, we would have to study dozens of separate issues among hundreds of people— far too many people for intensive interviews. But, in the words of Murphy (1987, p. 176): "It's back to questionnaires and the shallow data of survey research, and this is what I refuse to do." We preferred to have the emotional flavor of what people expressed in an unstructured interview, despite its limitations. We make no claims beyond their words and our impressions.

STRENGTHS

Having spelled out the limitations of these data, let me briefly describe our approach and its strengths. We carefully tape-recorded and transcribed all interviews, which averaged two two-hour interviews per person. At least two different interviewers reviewed these transcripts repeatedly. Then I studied all the transcripts, looking for emergent themes.

Because we wanted to capture relatives' subjective experiences, we did not overstructure the interviews.

> Our need to reduce all our data to a tidy system is just as much an attempt to cope with the sensory chaos of a world we do not fully understand as an exercise in science and it is subject to the same errors and uncertainties. [Murphy (1987), p. 176]

We asked people to tell us their stories in their words. Our opening question was: "Can you tell me what *your* experience has been with having a mentally ill [spouse, sibling, grandchild, parent, nephew, etc.] in the family?" To address our major hypotheses, we did ask about specific demographic data and some key questions. At the end of our open-ended interviews, we turned to our written guidelines to make sure all topics had been covered. If not, we asked about any remaining topics.

Without exception, our interviewees were eager to talk and needed little prompting. Most said they found it helpful to talk. They also liked being in the role of our teachers and contributing to our understanding of SMI's impact on the family.

At the close of all interviews, we offered people information about the National Alliance for the Mentally Ill, its local AMI chapter, the local mental health center, and articles to read on SMI, if they so desired. We answered questions and offered information.

SUMMARY

A 1992 study (Carpentier et al.) found that psychological distress was equally high for families living with or living away from their SMI relatives. We found this to be true with some family members who had never even met their SMI relatives. There was a skeleton in their closet that cast a dark shadow.

> The stigmatized family member suffers . . .
> but so do the parents, sisters and brothers,
> aunts and uncles, grandmothers and grand-
> fathers. [E. Fuller Torrey (1988), p. xiii]

Our intention was to understand this better, and that is what we set out to do.

A subjective element exists in all research by humans on humans. The greatest risk is in believing we know more than we do. My subjective bias and those of some of the student interviewers were increased by the fact that we are members of a family with a SMI relative. In contrast, we also had insider knowledge that can be very helpful. We had credibility with our interviewees, and we had good ideas about what questions to ask. Our sympathies were squarely with the family members. They have suffered a great deal and on the whole have been excluded by professionals who work with SMI. They sensed our understanding, and I believe this helped us get good data.

We are still a far cry from being able to draw conclusions about family members who suffer the ripple effects of having SMI in the family. This study is part of a process in which we hear from many different voices and try to understand their different perspectives. It is a beginning. Our common agony is that we can do so little to alleviate the terrible sufferings of people with severe mental illness. Medications usually relieve some symptoms, good community care can keep most people from being locked up most of the time, and education about SMI can reduce some of the stigma. But let us be honest with ourselves: the tortures of hallucinations, the failure to connect with people, and the anxieties, desperate isolation, and loneliness of people with serious mental illness take a staggering toll. There are things we can do, however, and one of these is to remain loyal for the long haul. The place in our hearts is as big as ever, though we often do not know what to say or do. But we have not abandoned, you, beloved, and we never will.

References

Carpentier, N., Lesage, A., Goulet, J., Lalonde, P., & Renaud, M. (1992). Burden of care for families not living with young schizophrenic relatives. *Hospital and Community Psychiatry, 43*, 38–43.

Mishler, E. G. (1986). *Research interviewing: Context and narrative.* Cambridge, MA: Harvard University Press.

Murphy, R. F. (1987). *The body silent.* New York: Norton.

Torrey, E. F. (1988). Preface. In J. Johnson, *Hidden victims* (p. xiii). New York: Doubleday.

II

CHILDREN:

"Help Me"

But my ultimate protection was
this: I was just passing through; a
guest in the house: perhaps this
wasn't my mother at all.
—Gloria Steinem (1983), p. 49

The past fifty years have seen a tremendous amount of
research about children with parents who have SMI, in contrast to
other family members. Articles have been written from every imaginable perspective, coming to every imaginable conclusion. This is
amusingly exemplified in a 1982 edition of the *Journal of Children
in Contemporary Society* which contains two conflicting opening
statements in different articles: "Much attention has recently been
given to the offspring of SMI parents" versus "Little attention has
been given to children of SMI parents."

Amusing items are scarce in this literature. Findings
consistently point in the direction of severe stress for the children.
To be the child of a parent with SMI is to have a confusing and
painful childhood. Common themes do emerge, both in the litera-

ture and in our twenty interviews. Three stand out as particularly interesting:

1. The striking contrast between vulnerable and seemingly invulnerable children
2. The enormous variation in coping strategies
3. The extent to which social services have ignored the plight of these children

This chapter summarizes the themes found in our interviews and in the post-1950 literature. It also discusses the variables found among children who seem to have survived comparatively well and suggests clinical interventions.

The Interviews

A few cautions must be mentioned in interpreting our interviews. To begin with, all our interviewees were adults recalling their pasts, and these memories, like all memories, are bound to be distorted and changed over time. Second, these twenty people were volunteers, white, and from the Midwest. For the most part, they all appeared to be functioning quite well. Although we undoubtedly have a biased sample, each person had fascinating and important things to report.

Every individual had different experiences, coping modalities, scars, and strengths. The enormous variations were impressive, but a few common themes emerged among people's experiences:

A sense of having no control over their lives' circumstances
Having no time for childhood, because they had to grow up fast
Role confusion or role reversal with the SMI parent
Loneliness

Anger, coupled with genetic fears (fears of
inheriting the illness)

Another characteristic of all our interviewees was their
eagerness to be heard. They wanted to tell their stories. To give you
a feel for the broad range of these adult children's experiences, a
random sample of their vignettes follows. Of course, as mentioned,
they were all volunteers. We do not know the stories of those who
remain silent.

One fifty-eight-year-old man said his mother had become SMI right
after his birth. Both the professionals involved and his relatives had
decided (between 1932 and 1952) that it was in his best interest to
keep him entirely away from his mother, and thus he was twenty
years old before he met her for the first time. "I was a kid without a
mother—all a big mystery to me."

At least three circumstances worked in this man's favor:
a stable and loving father, a grandmother who also helped raise
him, and his love for mathematics. "I was fascinated by math and
could get lost in it. It was my big escape." This illustrated a common
finding in our study and in the literature: those children who were
bright and had a strong interest in something outside the family
seemed to derive solace, satisfaction, and healthy escape from their
troubles.

After meeting her, this man visited his mother once or
twice a year until her death. Meanwhile, he became a successful
mathematician, husband, and father. Of his mother's mental illness, he says, "I feel such a terrible sense of tragedy for her."

In sharp contrast is the story of a twenty-two-year-old woman
whose parents both had SMI, as did many of her siblings and extended family members. Not only was she exposed to SMI from the
moment of birth, but because she was the sturdiest member of the
family, she took care of everybody from a very early age. As far back
as she can remember—which was age five, while in kindergarten—
she got meals on the table, cleaned her clothes for school, and
created some semblance of order in the chaotic household. Parenting her parents and other siblings, she had an enormous sense of

responsibility growing up; and she currently fears having to care for many relatives in the future. "I have a real tough time hanging on to my own sanity. It could happen to me any time. Mentally ill people shouldn't be allowed to have children."

This young woman told us she felt like an abused child and could remember feeling suicidal as early as age nine. "I always wanted out of my family." Lots of social workers dealt with the family over the years, but she said none of them ever told her anything or asked her what she wanted. "I hate social services for not helping me."

Miraculously, this woman has survived and is now a professional. How? We do not know for sure, of course, but she lists three factors that make sense. She had a cousin who took her in to live when she was fourteen years old. She successfully escaped into a lot of daydreaming. She was bright, did well in school, and was liked by her teachers. Again, we see the common themes of high intelligence, outside interests, and significant other adults. To this list of survival attributes, I would add what appears to be an innate mental sturdiness.

We interviewed two siblings (one thirty-two years old, the other forty-two) who had had totally different experiences from each other. They had lived at home with their mentally ill mother during very different stages of her illness. The forty-two-year-old had been there during a very active, loud, disruptive stage; the thirty-two-year-old had lived through bedridden, negative-symptom years of quiet withdrawal. As a result, these two siblings have difficulty understanding each other's view of their mother and of the home situation. This is probably a common phenomenon among different family members.

A twenty-seven-year-old man said of his father, who had been diagnosed with paranoid schizophrenia, "He was mentally ill all of my life, I think. His side of the family still doesn't admit it; they blame my mother for his illness." His father, an academic, committed suicide on the day of his son's college graduation. "I was so angry with him for that for about two years. This was followed by a great sadness. Now I just respect him for holding on as well as he did." He said on the topic of genetic fear: "It is always there." Now married, this man is following in his father's footsteps as an academic. He attributes his comparatively good survival to his mother, who always kept him well informed about SMI, and to a significant male friend of the family, who spent a lot of quality time with him. (Note again: high intelligence, outside interests, and significant adults as factors in a good outcome.)

From rural areas where community care was nil, we interviewed a twenty-year-old woman whose mother had a rather sudden onset of paranoid schizophrenia at age forty-four. The psychotic episode was violent and terrible. "She was screaming out of control and the whole household was in an uproar. We were terrified and called the police, who handcuffed her and took her to the hospital." There she was treated with medications in the emergency room and sent home, though the family begged the doctor to keep her. "We were not told what was wrong, or how to care for her. Jesus, we didn't know what end was up!" The husband and two daughters were afraid to leave her alone and took turns around the clock staying with her.

Their extended family was very upset, with everyone blaming everyone else. Ignorance, fear, and anger reigned. Relatives withdrew. The immediate family sought out a general practitioner who suggested it was "probably the menopause." At the time of our interview, this daughter still believed that this was the likely explanation. (An extra hour was spent after the interview to give her information, materials to read, and the phone number for AMI. The young woman said she was relieved by the information.)

The family could not keep up their constant watch. Left alone one hour, this forty-four-year-old woman committed suicide. At the time of our interview, her twenty-year-old daughter was in psychotherapy and "feeling stronger for it."

A different story came from a thirty-year-old man whose mother had been mentally ill all her life. He described himself at age seven as already in the business of raising a four-year-old brother. "My mom would lie upstairs in bed, crying all morning, and I knew that wasn't normal." Once when his mother attempted suicide, his father ordered him never to tell anyone. He told us he had felt insecure and frightened all his life. School, where he did well, was his salvation. We asked what other coping mechanisms he had used, and he mentioned turning to friends, writing, and getting drunk.

This man was not married and did not like the genetic/ biological theories of SMI, because they added to the fear of telling people. "I would never tell a date that my mother had SMI." (Again, our interviewer took the time to give information about genetic probabilities and answer this man's questions.)

We talked with a forty-seven-year-old woman whose mother had been ill for thirty years. "Mental illness and unpredictability ruled the house. Life centered about trying not to upset her." When asked who or what helped her cope during her adolescent years, she said her grandparents. When her father died, our interviewee became guardian of her mother and placed her in a nursing facility right away. "This pulled all the scabs off my pain. Oh, I felt so guilty." Now, a few years later, she visits her mother once a month.

A twenty-three-year-old woman talked about being seventeen when her father developed an SMI. With great anger, she recalled her one experience with professionals: "We had one family therapy session behind a one-way mirror with people gawking at us. I just hated it. They didn't even tell us what SMI was. They were just probing our psyches." As she described it, the therapy session did one good thing for the family: "We hated it so much that it pulled us together as a family."

It is hard to stop writing these vignettes from our interviews. People all told their stories with deep feeling and an eagerness to be heard, as well as the desire to contribute to knowledge about children who have parents with SMI.

SUMMARY OF INTERVIEWS

These children's intelligence and ability to see that their parent had an illness, rather than blaming themselves, played a role in their survival. So did other significant adults and outside interests. These are the same themes found in the literature, lending credibility to both the literature and our findings.

Other themes that stood out were the abilities to withdraw successfully into reading, writing, and daydreaming. Interviewees commonly expressed feelings of being set apart from other people: "Mental illness steals from a person; you are not like others." All our interviewees reported childhoods pervaded by a sense of lacking control: "Things just happened." They also wondered about the lack of help from professionals, and quite a few were now in therapy.

The dominant regret as they looked back into their pasts was that there had been no room for their problems. All conversations, energy, and efforts were directed to the problems of the parent with SMI. Whether or not this was always the case, we have no way of knowing; but it was surely their memory and perception of the situation. The most frequent present feeling expressed was sadness: a poignant sadness for the tragedy and waste of their parents' lives, and also for their own lost childhoods.

It is tempting to try to find a common motif for their future concerns, but the variation we found was too great to make any claims. We marveled at the struggles and strengths of our twenty interviewees.

The Literature

The ensuing section briefly reviews some dominant themes and findings of the past thirty years, some trends in professional thought, and what are presently considered high-risk factors for the children of SMI parents. The next section suggests ways of easing some of their stresses and damages.

LITERATURE FROM PROFESSIONALS

Earlier literature on children with SMI parents focused on very disturbed children (e.g., Rutter, 1979). An example of this is Anthony's (1968, 1969) work. In an extensive clinical study of six- to twelve-year-old children of psychotic parents, he found a number of clinical disturbances in these children, including withdrawal, mistrustfulness, and some delusions and hallucinations. The 10 to 20 percent of the children who displayed no signs of pathology were said to have "brittle normalcy," suggesting abnormality even in normalcy. Anthony (1969) claimed that separation from the sick parent seemed to have little value in preventing psychotic episodes. This claim points in the direction of biological causes as well as environmental.

Two commonly cited researchers are Mednick and Schulsinger (1975), who conducted a series of studies in Denmark. They compared 207 high-risk children with schizophrenic mothers to 104 low-risk children whose parental figures had no mental illness. Of the high-risk group, 9 percent manifested schizophrenia and 32 percent showed borderline states such as schizoid or paranoid personalities. For the low-risk group, the respective percentages were 1 and 4. Only 15 percent of the high-risk group showed no mental disorder.

Many studies investigate the incidence of pathology and emotional disorders in children of parents with mental illness (e.g., Garmezy, 1971; Goodman, 1984; Grunebaum & Cohler, 1982). Various findings have been contradictory, and studies are often limited by small samples and lack of standardized procedures. Many studies contend that children with parents who have SMI are at high risk of pathology. However, some studies have reported no increase in maladjustment or symptomatology for such offspring.

Much of the research reported in the 1960s and 1970s attempted to determine how much and what kinds of pathology children inherit from their parents. After diagnosing abnormality, researchers intended to learn whether that pathology was transmitted through genetic influences or the "psychotic environment."

On the positive side, this research helped solidify that schizophrenia and other serious mental illnesses have a genetic, biochemical component. This research also acknowledged that children were in a high-risk category.

Also emerging then was *high-risk research* and research on stress-resistant children. Garmezy (1971) explained high-risk research as studying vulnerable children to discover precursors to later pathology. The focus thus shifted from the study of pathology to include prevention and intervention. Asarnow (1988) hoped to separate what went on before the disorder from secondary deficits caused by the disorder, so that SMI could possibly be prevented in vulnerable children.

Interest in risk research and possible prevention seemed to stem from evidence that many children of parents with SMI do not develop emotional disturbances. Garmezy (1971) cited research by Mednick and Schulsinger (1968) which stated that 12 to 14 percent of high-risk children will develop some form of schizophrenic disorder, while 35 percent will manifest some other form of atypical behavior. Garmezy converted this data to show that approximately 50 percent of these children will be functioning adequately and symptom-free (1971). Garmezy called these people "invulnerable children," instead of using Anthony's (1968) term of "brittle normalcy." (In 1987 he changed his terminology from "invulnerable" to "stress-resistant" children.) In 1974 Garmezy argued against the profession's preoccupation with pathology and suggested looking at how people adapt in the face of adversity. This represented an important philosophical change. It acknowledges the large number of children who do not show signs of pathology or serious maladjustment.

The notions of "invulnerable children" as well as the "vulnerable children" attracted research to isolate *protective factors*: circumstances that help people resist the potentially negative influences of parental mental illness. Mednick (1973) studied forty children with mothers who had SMI, twenty of whom experienced "breakdown" and twenty of whom did not. Mednick discovered that the "non-breakdown" children experienced the loss of their mothers at a later age and acquired substitute mothers more frequently than did children of the breakdown group. The former also had fathers who were healthy and available.

Rutter (1979) identified six familial risk factors seemingly correlated with childhood psychiatric disorders: severe marital distress, low social status, overcrowding or large family size, paternal criminality, maternal psychiatric disorders, and placing children into foster homes. Rutter also identified some protective factors:

1. The establishment of at least one stable child–adult relationship
2. A stable and cohesive family climate
3. The acquisition of cognitive and social skills that help survival during stress. (Rutter stated that a positive school environment can help nourish such competencies in a child.)

More recently, the Emory University Project also identified some protective factors. These include: higher educational level of the parent with SMI, work experience of that parent, and the presence of other relatives to help with child care (Goodman, 1987).

This new focus on prevention provided the base for professionals to start designing intervention programs for high-risk children and parents with mental illness.

CLINICAL INTERVENTIONS

Goodman and Isaacs (1984) stated three general goals for interventions with children of psychiatrically ill parents: to improve family stability, to foster the mother's ability to meet the child's needs, and to minimize the pathology to which the child is exposed. Many researchers have commented on ways to meet these goals. Silverman (1989) offered one basic prevention strategy: to identify and treat parental mental illness early, before the family and children are as affected negatively. This strategy would require increased mental-health facilities and easy access. Silverman also called for increased education and training for family members. He stated that awareness of the illness and their vulnerabilities allows family members to develop specific coping skills and resistances to the effects of parental psychopathology.

Cohler and Musick (1984) stressed the importance of developing children's coping skills so that they can reach out to healthy adults and find alternative environments that partly diminish contact with the chaotic home. They suggested support programs that help the child develop hobbies and become interested in school, increased use of self-help groups, and reliance on natural neighborhood social networks. Silverman (1989) added that schools should foster social competence, encourage peer counseling, and provide support for students undergoing transitions. Goodman and Isaacs (1984) also emphasized teaching the child coping skills and problem solving, and having strong social support networks in place.

Silverman (1989) cited a paper by Goldstein (1978) that suggests three preventive targets: special attention to prenatal nutrition, prenatal counseling, and postnatal bonding; teaching children problem-solving and social skills in middle childhood; and addressing patterns of communication within family units. Silverman also commented that supportive family and community systems are important. Employment opportunities, strong natural kinship with other healthy relatives, parental care, and access to high-quality child care and education exemplify ways to protect children and the family.

In addition to these general suggestions, specific programs have been designed for parents with a mental illness and their children. There are basically two kinds of programs: *child-centered*: primarily concerned with support for the child, not necessarily the larger family unit; and *family-focused*: designed on the assumption that helping the parent will help the child and the family.

Marsh (1992) pointed out that while a good deal of literature is concerned with the experience of children, we have little understanding of their lifetime development with these experiences. That is, children at different ages are going through their own life cycles, and all kinds of developmental crises may develop. A six-year-old whose mother is being hospitalized just as he starts first grade may feel betrayed by her, suffer severe separation anxiety, or develop a school phobia. A most significant variable is the age of the child when the parent develops or is in crisis with SMI. Obviously, it will make a big difference if the child's age is six months, ten years, or nineteen years.

Marsh also wrote about the *parentification* that sometimes occurs as the child tries to help out by taking over: "children may deny themselves healthy opportunities for rebellion in their effort to protect their already overburdened parents" (p. 123). She talked about "serious guilt," and the "dual risks of enmeshment and disengagement" that almost always confront "children who struggle to incorporate the mental illness of a family member into their own lives" (p. 124). Children are in a constant struggle to maintain normalcy in the face of abnormal and unpredictable crises. Marsh recommended attending to the child's developmental life cycle when planning interventions.

Sturges (1971, 1977) discussed ways to talk with children. She touched on various feelings that children may have when a parent is hospitalized. To explain the child's emotional reality, she used descriptive words such as "frightened, confused, relief, guilt, grieving, role changes, resentment, turbulence, unhappiness and disruption." She urged family members and others to talk with children about SMI and to include them in any therapeutic process, because information about the mental illness aids in coping. Reminding us that a child's fantasies may be much worse than reality, she wrote that the child may not feel comfortable raising questions in an already stressful environment. Questions of fault and responsibility should be addressed, and children need to understand that they are not to blame.

Sturges listed idiosyncratic roles that children tend to take on in response to parental mental illness:

1.   *Caretaker*: Some children respond by caring for the ill parent or a sibling, especially younger siblings.

2. *Baby*: Some children regress to a clinging, whining, demanding state, become fearful of going to school or playing with friends, and may develop separation anxieties.
3. *Mourner*: A child may demonstrate excessive and prolonged grief, may cry often and refuse to eat, or may develop chronic depression.
4. *Patient*: A child may develop somatic symptoms, become depressed, act like the ill family member, and may actually become psychotic.
5. *Escapee*: Children who adopt this role manage anxiety with overactivity and involvement in activities away from the family, often avoid family members, and may move out of the home.
6. *Recluse*: Some children withdraw from peers, school, and family; may isolate in their own room; and feel embarrassment about explaining a family member's illness to others.
7. *Good child*: In this role, the child becomes extremely well behaved, assuming tasks he or she never wanted to do before, and doing whatever possible to avoid conflict within the family. The good child may be atoning for guilt or trying to minimize stress at home.
8. *Bad child*: A child may become openly angry, hostile, or defiant; and may act out through delinquency, drug or alcohol abuse, or promiscuity.

Anthony (1975) identified some emotional consequences for children with a mentally ill parent. He noted that many children displayed hopelessness, insecurity, lack of self-confidence, and low self-esteem. He described a child's response to a parent's hospitalization as similar to the mourning cycle of protest–despair–detachment (1973). This can create feelings of alienation and/or abandonment, intense rage, and despair. Anthony suggested teaching children coping methods through individual therapy and group counseling.

Bernheim (1982) introduced *supportive family counseling* for people who are dealing with mental illness. (This differs from the family therapy model, which assumes that disturbances in the family have caused the illness.) Its goals are to provide information, emotional support, and recognition that individual family members have their own needs. The counselor's methods include developing a therapeutic alliance with the family, communicating acceptance, educating the family, helping members set realistic expectations about their relative with SMI, and helping them handle day-to-day problems.

Using children's fiction is another means of helping young children cope with parental mental illness. Sargent (1985) felt that stories can help children understand mental illness, model acceptance of substitute parenting and extended family, present coping skills, portray healthy peer relationships, and describe other environments in which children function normally despite the negative nature of a parent's mental illness. After reviewing children's literature, Sargent recommended four children's stories that she deemed useful in working with children: *Celebrate the Morning* (Ellis, 1972), *The Night Birds* (Haugen, 1982), *Stranger in the House* (Sherburne, 1963), *Toby Lived Here* (Wolitzer, 1980), and *Is Dad Crazy?* (Liddicut, 1989).

De Chillo et al. (1987) reviewed the literature to better understand the following questions: Do we incorporate what we know of children of mentally ill parents into treatment of the parents? Do we even get information about the children? How often are children included in the service delivery? What is the nature of the social worker's contact with the children? Are children at risk for behavior disturbance? If so, are they provided with help? Their review showed that:

- A specific diagnosis of the ill parent is less important to the child than the mental health of the nonhospitalized parent, and the involvement of that parent with the child.
- The child who gets drawn into the psychosis of the parent is distinct from the child who manages to see the parent as clearly ill and can separate sufficiently from the ill parent.
- Although the disturbances of a psychotic parent might frighten a child, the apathy of a depressed parent can be even more deleterious to a child.

- Studies of bright, talented children have shown that extensive positive contact with an extrafamilial adult or best friend is an important protective factor. Also, a warm relationship with an ill parent can occur despite severe pathology. Such a connection can cause less distress and even foster extra competence in the child.
- Children of unipolar (depressed) parents seem more impaired than children of bipolar ("Manic-depressive") parents.
- Depressed mothers have trouble meeting children's needs and setting limits for them.
- The presence of other people in the child's environment is protective and helpful, even when the parental illness is chronic, if those people can provide reality checks and validate the child's sense that something is wrong with the SMI parent.
- Spouses of mentally ill individuals can become depressed themselves while caregiving, further depriving the child of needed support.
- Younger children exposed to an ill parent suffer attentional problems and separation difficulties, lowered initiative, and withdrawal; latency-age children exhibit more behavioral disturbance.
- High school dropout rates are greater for adolescent offspring of mentally ill parents than those of other ill parents.
- Inpatient hospital records showed that social workers often are unaware that a SMI patient had any offspring, or do not know the children's whereabouts.*

Stiffman, Jung and Feldman (1988) pointed out that research has rarely examined how living arrangements affect the behavior of children with mentally ill parents. Their study evaluated the family environment, behavior, and skills of 306 children with mentally ill parents and examined the relationship between these

---

* New York State now mandates that hospitals routinely check with patients to see if they have children at home.

variables and various living arrangements. Alternative living arrangements, such as foster care or care from relatives, correlated with better child behavior and a lower level of family discord. They concluded that a reevaluation is needed of child welfare policies aimed at maintaining biological family integrity at all costs, with respect to children living with mentally ill parents.

Stories from our interviews, as well as literature written by adult children, also leave me seriously questioning our present policies of trying to maintain an intact family at all costs. It looks like the cost is too high in many cases. It is also not easy to determine what the best policy would be.

LITERATURE FROM ADULT CHILDREN

Reading books and articles by people whose parents had SMI brings another valuable dimension to our understanding.

> Only then could I end the terrible calm that comes with crises and admit to myself how afraid I had been.
> —Gloria Steinem, (1983), p. 50

Lanquetot (1988) wrote a very moving personal account, "On Being Daughter and Mother," in the *Schizophrenia Bulletin*. As a child, she resented having a mother with SMI, and grandparents who asked that she look after her mother. Many years later, Lanquetot had a son who developed schizophrenia. Of this tragedy she writes: "If I were granted one wish, I'd wish for my son's [recovery], but if that wish could not be granted, I'd wish for a grandchild to take my place to care for my son after my death" (p. 341).

In another first-person account, Crosby (1989) remembered feeling a desperate denial of anything being wrong. As a child, "I was aware of her paranoia, and I was aware it was not based on facts" (p. 508). People withdrew from the family, no visitors ever came to the house. "It was just we two little girls with our mother who was slipping further and further away from us and, more importantly, from reality" (p. 508). There was no time for childhood; she had to be responsible, tough, and brave. The father and two children would cry but never talk about it, as it was much too painful.

Crosby described how she tried hard not to love her mother, because that was anguishing. She ended her article with: "I have been gifted with the rediscovery of my love for my mother . . . setting aside the broken heart I have been carrying around within me. I love my mother just as she is" (p. 508).

Feeling a strong sense of responsibility at a young age is a common theme in writings by adult children. Lanquetot (1984) writes, "Trying to make up for my mother's shortcomings was one of the major preoccupations of my years. I was always cleaning and straightening up the house, vainly hoping to restore order, even as early as age 4. I took care of my brothers, but I bitterly resented the fact that no one took care of me." Many children described a terrible sense of early responsibility which affected their entire family, and devastated their adolescence.

Lefley (1985) surveyed eighty-four mental health workers who have a family member with SMI. Eighteen of the workers were adult children, and the other sixty-six were parents of mentally ill children. Most of the adult children said that mental health workers did not recognize the extent of their pain or their burden in dealing with the SMI parent.

The literature from adult children matched what we heard in our interviews. Their confusion, pain, and fear were loud and clear. My guess is that we are hearing from only those adult children who survived relatively intact. Are they a fraction of all adult children with SMI parents? Or the majority? Or somewhere in between? Not enough is known to venture a guess at this point.

Conclusion

Over twenty years ago, Garmezy (1971, p. 111) researched so-called invulnerable children.

> These "invulnerable children" remain the
> "keepers of the dream." Were we to study the
> forces that move such children to survival
> and adaptation, the long range benefits to
> our society might be more significant than
> our many efforts . . . designed to curtail the
> incidence of vulnerability.

Since then, studies have revealed less psychopathology than
expected from the highly stressful environments in which these
children were raised. Children who do comparatively well appear
to be able to selectively ignore parental pathology and to take
advantage of other adults as caretakers and teachers (Sargent,
1985).

   Other findings on children who did well were that they
had: resistance to being engulfed by the illness, intellectual curiosity
plus high intelligence, and someone who gave them information
about SMI. Shannon (1988) found it also helped if experiences in
the home offered the child a sense of purpose and a sense of
achievement. An example she gave was children who felt they were
successful in protecting themselves, a sibling, or a parent. Anthony
(1968) wrote of children who survive well as having a lack of
vulnerability, the capacity for adaptation and coping, active mastery
skills, and an understanding that it is the parent who is ill rather than
the child who is at fault. It is not clear whether Anthony saw these as
innate capacities or as capacities fostered by environmental circumstances. As in most things, it is probably a combination of both.

   Whether or not children survive comparatively well,
their experiences are very difficult. People with SMI are unpredictable, and children report feelings of having a parent who is
there but not there. All the literature—both from professionals and
adult children—and our interviews used the same words to describe the children's experiences: frightened, confused, guilty, grief,
role changes, too much responsibility, resentment, disruption, turbulence, depression, neglect, deprivation, anxiety, and frustration.
Not a pretty picture.

   Another big problem for children, especially when they
are young, is that they view the sick behavior as intentional rather

than as part of the illness. Teenage children often express "survivor's guilt" and the fear of abandoning their parents if they leave home. They also have genetic fears for themselves.

Most people, especially children and teenagers, want to appear normal and want to come from the idealized "Normal" Rockwell–type family. Marsh (1992, p.123) writes, "[The children of SMI parents] may also join other family members in retreating from the anguish and pain, as the family invests heavily in a facade of normalcy."

Disruptions in child care resulting from hospitalization of the parent, in addition to poor parenting, have serious impact on children. Furthermore, children who expect the parent to come home "cured" are confused and disappointed when that does not happen. Based on the foregoing findings, it is abundantly clear that these children are badly in need of care, attention, and information. Thus far, the community mental health movement has neglected the needs of children. That movement's prime efforts have centered on avoiding hospitalization of people with SMI.

The few examples we have of early intervention with children show positive results. An example of this is the Thresholds Mothers project in Chicago, a demonstration project funded by the National Institute of Mental Health. This day-treatment program for mothers with SMI and their children includes active outreach and home care. Outcome measures show significant improvement for both mothers and children.

Checklist

We need greater collaboration among mental health centers, child welfare agencies, the educational and juvenile justice systems, and the churches and temples. Based on what we know, the following seem important:

1. Children need adequate substitute child care.
2. Children need to be told, repeatedly, that they are not to blame for the parent's illness.

3. They need information about SMI. This cannot be a "one-shot deal." Children need ongoing education and reassurance until such time as they can continue to learn on their own.
4. They need guidance in learning new ways to think about and cope with the parent with SMI.
5. Children need encouragement and support for interests and activities outside the home. This should include every possible resource for success at school.

> Intimate attachments to other human beings are the hub around which a person's life revolves ... from these intimate attachments a person draws his strength and enjoyment of life and, through what he contributes he gives strength and enjoyment to others. These are matters about which current science and traditional wisdom are one.
> —Bowlby (1980), p. 442

Indeed, the research, our interviews, and the literature written by children with SMI parents all seem to be "at one."

References

Anthony, E. J. (1968). The developmental precursors of adult schizophrenia. *Journal of Psychiatric Research, 6* (Supp. 1), 293–316.

Anthony, E. J. (1974). A risk-vulnerability intervention model for children of psychotic parents. In E. J. Anthony & C. Koupernik (Eds.), *The child in his family: Children at psychiatric risk, Vol. 3* (pp. 99–122). New York: Wiley.

Anthony, E. J. (1975). The influence of a manic-depressive environment on the developing child. In E. J. Anthony & T. Benedek (Eds.), *Depression and human existence* (pp. 279–315). Boston: Little, Brown.

Asarnow, J. R. (1988). Children at risk for schizophrenia: Converging lines of evidence. *Schizophrenia Bulletin, 14*(4), 613–631.

Bernheim, K. F. (1982). Supportive family counseling. *Schizophrenia Bulletin, 8,* 634–641.

Bowlby, J. (1980). *Loss, sadness and depression.* New York: Basic Books.

Cohler, B. J., & Musick, J. S. (1984). Editors' notes. (Special issue:) Intervention among psychiatrically impaired parents and their young children. *New Directions for Mental Health Services, 24,* 1–5.

Crosby, K. D. (1989). First-person account: Growing up with a schizophrenic mother. *Schizophrenia Bulletin, 15*(3), 507–509.

DeChillo, N., Matorin, S., & Hallahan, C. (1987). Children of psychiatric patients: Rarely seen or heard. *Health and Social Work, 12,* 296–302.

Ellis, A. (1972). Celebrate the morning. In K. Sargent (1985), Helping children cope with parental mental illness through use of children's literature. *Child Welfare, 64*(51), 617–629.

Garmezy, N. (1971). Vulnerability research and the issue of primary prevention. *American Journal of Orthopsychiatry, 4,* 101–115.

32   *The Skipping Stone*

Garmezy, N. (1987). Stress, competence, and development: Con-
tinuities in the study of schizophrenic adults, children
vulnerable to psychopathology, and the search for stress-
resistant children. *American Journal of Orthopsychiatry,
57,* 159–174.

Goodman, S. H. (1984). Children of emotionally disturbed mothers:
Problems and alternatives. *Children Today, 1392,* 6–9.

Goodman, S. H. (1987). Emory University project on children of
disturbed parents. *Schizophrenia Bulletin, 13,* 412–
423.

Goodman, S. H., & Isaacs, L. D. (1984). Primary prevention with
children of severely disturbed mothers. *Journal of Preventive Psychiatry, 2,* 387–402.

Grunebaum, H., & Cohler, B. J. (1982). Children of parents hospitalized for mental illness. *Journal of Children in Contemporary Society, 15*(1), 43–55.

Grunebaum, H., Weiss, J., Cohler, B., Hartman, C., & Gallant, D.
(Eds.). (1982). *Mentally ill mothers and their children.*
Chicago: Chicago University Press.

Hatfield, A. (1981). Coping effectiveness in the families of the
mentally ill: An exploratory study. *Journal of Psychiatric
Treatment and Evaluation, 3,* 11–19.

Haugen, R. (1982). *The night birds.* Translated by Sheila La Forge.
New York: Delacorte.

Lanquetot, E. (1984). First-person account: Confessions of the
daughter of a schizophrenic. *Schizophrenia Bulletin,
10*(3), 467–471.

Lanquetot, R. (1988). First-person account: On being daughter
and mother. *Schizophrenia Bulletin, 14*(2), 337–341.

Lefley, H. P. (1985). Etiological and prevention views of clinicians
with mentally ill relatives. *American Journal of Orthopsychiatry, 55*(3), 363–370.

Liddicut, J. (1989). *Is dad crazy?* Victoria, Australia: Schizophrenia
Australia Foundation.

Marsh, D. T. (1992). *Families and mental illness: New directions in
professional practice.* New York: Praeger Publishing.

Mednick, S., Schulsinger, H., & Schulsinger, F. (1973). Schizophrenia in children of schizophrenic mothers. In A.

Davids (Ed.), *Child personality and psychopathology* (Vol 2). New York: Willey.

Ranjan, R. (1990–91). Genetic counseling for schizophrenia. *British Journal of Psychiatry, 147,* 107–112.

Rolf, J. & Harig, P. (1974). Etiological research in schizophrenia and the rationale for primary intervention. *American Journal of Orthopsychiatry, 44,* 539–554.

Rutter, M. (1979). Protective factors in children's responses to stress and disadvantage. In M. W. Kent & J. Rold (Eds.), *Primary Prevention of Psychopathology: Social Competence in Children* (Vol. 3). Hanover, NH: University Press of New England.

Sargent, K. (1985). Helping children cope with parental mental illness through use of children's literature. *Child Welfare, 64,* 617–629.

Shannon, M. (1988). Adult children of schizophrenic parents. Letter to the editor. *Schizophrenia Bulletin, 14*(4), 495–596.

Sherburne, Z. (1963). *Stranger in the house.* New York: William Morrow.

Silverman, M. M. (1989). Children of psychiatrically ill parents: A prevention perspective. *Hospital and Community Psychiatry, 4*(12), 1257–1265.

Steinem, G. (1983). Ruth's song. *Ms. Magazine, 46*(Sept.), 47–50, 73–77.

Stiffman, A. R., Jung, K. G., & Feldman, R. A. (1988). Parental mental illness, family living arrangements, and child behavior. *Journal of Social Service Research, 11* (2–3), 21–34.

Sturges, J. S. (1977). Children's reactions to mental illness in the family. *Social Casework,* Nov., 530–536.

Sturges, J. S. (1971). Talking with children about mental illness. *Health and Social Work, 2,* 87–109.

Sturges, J. S. (1977). Children's reactions to mental illness in the family. *Social Casework, 59,* 530–536.

Wolitzer, H. (1980). *Toby lived here.* New York: Bantam Books.

III

SIBLINGS:

"Please Hear Me"

William Tell

My brother William tells me of our childhood. He was called Billy, and sometimes still is. He has a brown eye like the color of chestnuts; a blue/green eye not unlike my own, unlike my own. He is thirty.

His world is two parts in one song sung of dissident chords and the melancholy tunes hummed by old men playing chess. William tells me of our bond and our mutual home-spun harvest of memories. They reach out with his large hand, calling me along and comforting my own adult aloneness. The blue/green eye homes my brother. The brown eye homes a homeless wind walker. A specter of a man who could never be. Like a lost soul who refuses to accept its passing. William walks in dark lands.

My brother William tells me of his awake nightmares. Holds me as when we were chil-

dren and cries for our Mother now dead
these seven years. The brown eyed man is
with me. I wait and am mother/sister to the
little boy in his other eye who cannot understand *WHY* this is his fate, his torture. The
brown eyed man bullies my small brother ... I
sit and wait for Bill to draw them together. He
sleeps. He starts. In the darkness he cries out
and all I can do is sit waiting out the demons
with him; waiting for his butterflies.

William tells me about myself. Who I have
been, who I do not wish to be. Who I cannot
escape becoming. Who I must grow up to be
for both of us. William, tell me, where do the
butterflies go? Where do we fly when there is
no day, or night to twilight? William, tell me a
story of what happens to the butterfly when he
goes to sleep by the brooks of your mind. . . .
                    —H. Devon Hansen-Chastain
                                        (1990)

The idea for this chapter started at the National Alliance
for the Mentally Ill (NAMI) Conference in 1990, at a morning
devoted to a Siblings Meeting. In a large room with about 150
siblings of mentally ill adults, ranging in age from their early teens to
their seventies, people were briefly telling their stories. Now it was
my turn. "I'm not a sibling," I said. "I'm a parent, though. Please, I
thought if I just listened quietly I could learn from you what my well
children do not tell me." I stayed, and what I learned took my breath
away.

My students and I later researched what little post-1960
literature we could find on siblings of the severely mentally ill. And a
few gifted graduate students and I did in-depth interviews (two to
four hours each) with twenty siblings.

This chapter reports our interview findings, reviews dominant themes in the literature from 1960 to 1992, and then describes some issues that emerged from both the literature and interviews. Finally, I make suggestions as to how mental health professionals and parents may be able to alleviate some of the pains and struggles of the well siblings.

The Interviews

We interviewed siblings whose ages ranged from nineteen to seventy-two. The variability among them was enormous. We talked with teenagers who had never known their respective SMI siblings to be well, and a seventy-two-year-old woman who had been married with children of her own when her brother became ill. Some people were in their first year of coping; some, in their thirtieth. Our sample included agnostics and deeply religious people; siblings from close families and others from chaotic families. These and many other variables affect how an individual experiences the mental illness of his or her sibling.

FINDINGS: "PLEASE HEAR ME"

No generalizations about all siblings of people with SMI can be made from twenty interviews, but certain feelings consistently emerged: sadness, loss, and intense suffering. A few findings are consistent both within the literature by siblings and in our interviews. These are:

1. The desire to be heard
2. Genetic fears for either themselves or their children
3. The need for information about the mental illness

Genetic fears and the need for information go hand in hand. Severe mental illness has a genetic component, but it is relatively rarely shared among siblings. Information about the statistical probabilities for themselves and/or their children is thus helpful to siblings.

While 100 percent of our sample expressed genetic concerns, their responses covered the whole gamut from "I'd never have children" to wanting to have many children to make up for the loss of the sibling with severe mental illness. All interviewees described their adolescent years as fraught with worry about also going "crazy."

The whole idea behind our interviews was to *hear* from the siblings, so this theme may have been amplified—but we do not think so. These people's plea was quite strong, and their needs had been often overlooked. For many of our interviewees' parents, the disabled child and his or her needs became almost an obsession; any family gathering became consumed by talk about the mentally ill child and his or her problems, living arrangements, treatments, accomplishments, and failures. These families often minimized the feelings and experiences of the well siblings, who came to believe that their needs were irrelevant. A particularly poignant response came from a sibling who was telling his mother the news of his engagement to be married. His mentally ill brother, who was present, said: "It's funny . . . you're getting married, and I've never even had a girlfriend." Their mother's eyes filled with tears, and she turned away. "She was trying her best to be happy for me . . . ."

Another commonly expressed reason for not being heard was guilt—survivor's guilt. The unafflicted siblings knew their lives were better than those of their ill siblings, so how dare they complain? Discussions, crying, yelling, even the silences about the mentally ill child were painful. Yet silence was safest—anything not to upset their parents further. So avoiding the topic of their sibling's illness altogether seemed like the solution. Family extremes were secrecy and silence at one end, and obsessive concern on the other. Siblings seemed hurt by both, and neither alleviated their guilt.

Our interviewees were acutely aware of how much their parents were hurting. One young man stated: "It's not so much the relationship to our ill sibling that you need to know about, but rather how this illness affects all our other relationships in the family."

When asked for examples, he said: "Look, I kept silent on any issue I might have had with my parents or anyone else. We had enough problems because of [my brother]—I wasn't about to create any more."

This fits with what I observed at the NAMI Siblings Meeting: a roomful of high achievers trying to counterbalance the chaos and pain of their ill brothers and sisters. We do not know, of course, whether these same people might have been high achievers regardless. Nor do we know anything about the majority of siblings, who are not represented at NAMI meetings.

COPING WITH THE SYMPTOMS

Among siblings we interviewed, coping strategies varied a great deal over time. Because it usually takes years before a family knows what is going on with a "problem child," members may experience years of trouble before they get an accurate diagnosis. Even with a diagnosis, alas, many families are still left in the dark about the illness, its cause, its prognosis, and how best to handle behavioral problems. So the nightmare of not knowing—not knowing why their loved one has become ill, how they can best cope with the ill child, how they can cope with their own chaotic and sad feelings, and what community resources may be available to them—continues for years, and sometimes forever.

In the early stages of their siblings' illnesses, our interviewees expressed confusion, chaos, denial, and a desire to escape. "I'm out of here" was a phrase we heard often. Brothers and sisters also expressed secrecy and shame in the beginning—and for many, these feelings persisted throughout all stages of coping. With siblings who became ill during the 1970s, the peak of the drug counterculture, some people had attributed unusual behavior to the times: it was hip to drop out of school and take drugs, certain behaviors could be dismissed as drug induced, and SMI symptoms were thus masked.

Not all the people we interviewed were beyond the earliest stages of coping. Those who were—and for the most part, they were over age thirty—were owning up to the full impact of their sadness and grieving. One thirty-five-year-old woman said: "I'm beginning to love my ill brother for who he is now. I hope to stop grieving for the healthy brother he once was." These older siblings expressed more acceptance. They were coming to grips, however sadly, with their probable future roles as caretakers for their siblings after their parents' deaths. Some were already at that stage and shouldering their burden well.

One man described himself as "messing up my life to keep my brother healthy." He explained that as a teenager, he had figured if he did poorly in school and got in trouble with the law, he could keep his ill brother in the position of being his big brother. "I could get attention by getting just as sick as he was." One consistent experience among our sample was that younger siblings found it painful to surpass an older sibling with SMI. "I'm still dealing with trying to disguise the fact that I'm ahead of him now. I always looked up to him, and now it's in reverse."

Coping involved the desire to escape the pain and loss, and sometimes to continue the secrecy. Siblings described "vegging out on TV" as well as using drugs and alcohol to escape. Searching for answers, treatments, cures, and miracles were other commonly reported coping mechanisms. Another was guilt: "What did I do wrong to my brother [sister]?" As a way of allaying guilt, many siblings took on extra household responsibilities or pitched in during times of crisis.

A lot depended on how much information the siblings were getting. The more knowledge they had, the better their coping. Some of the more effective strategies were: seeking information from books, joining the Alliance for the Mentally Ill (AMI), meditating, and working through problems in therapy. Educating themselves about mental illness seemed the most effective coping strategy for these siblings.

To the question "How has your sibling's illness influenced your life?", we consistently got variations of "I survived!" For our interviewees, SMI's effects were dominated by pain—their own, that of their respective ill siblings, and that of their entire families.

Each sibling was well aware of the impact on the family. Here, too, we heard almost the full range, from "It blew us apart as a family" to "It brought us all closer together." We never heard a neutral stance, however.

Other frequently expressed effects were: "It helped me see the fragility of life"; "I've learned to be more tolerant; the future is an ever-present, painful thought—but I will take over when I have to"; "People who don't have severe mental illness in the family can't possibly know what it is like."

A word about professional help. Only two of our twenty interviewees had anything positive to say about professional contact with siblings. Most people described being neglected by professionals. When professionals had tried to help, these siblings had seen the interventions as harmful. Examples of this were "family bashing" that took place in family therapy, being locked up in the hospital with the patient for therapy, being videotaped in family therapy by a "show-off" therapist, and being refused information under the guise of confidentiality. The destructiveness of feeling blamed or of being kept in ignorance cannot be overestimated.

Conversely, we cannot underestimate the help that these siblings reported receiving from books, AMI and NAMI, and talking with people who understood their pain. We were deeply touched by the willingness and eagerness of all our volunteer interviewees to tell us their stories. They wanted to be heard.

Literature Review

After reviewing books and articles about siblings, we saw two obvious dimensions of the literature. One was chronological (since 1960). The other was authorship: professional research and accounts by the siblings. Not surprisingly, researchers slanted toward *causes of* stress, and siblings were and are more concerned with *reactions to* stress.

PROFESSIONAL RESEARCH

Professional literature from the 1960s is dominated by the psychodynamic theories of causality. The early research is highly speculative; in hindsight, it is easy to see researcher biases. In the work of Day and Kwitkowska (1962), for example, an art therapist and research psychiatrist compared the art work done by psychiatric patients and their well siblings. The authors' primary thesis was that although the siblings of psychiatric patients may "appear well," their mental health is superficial. This is an example of seeking solutions for serious mental illness by pathologizing family members. While observations made in this article may be accurate, they confuse cause and effect. The researchers also make generalizations based on very small samples. They see the behavior of the well siblings in terms of pathology rather than adaptation to and coping with trying circumstances.

In the nine years from 1963 to 1972, professional literature shifted from viewing the siblings as pathologiclly disturbed to seeing no significant differences between them and siblings of non–mentally ill people. For example, in 1963 Lidz claimed 75 percent of siblings in his study were "emotionally disturbed, borderline, or clinically schizophrenic." In 1969 Pollack et al. said that siblings' rates of psychopathology were significantly lower than those reported by Lidz. Finally, in 1972, Hoover and Franz compared siblings of schizophrenic people to normal college students without schizophrenic siblings and found no differences between the two groups' rates of psychopathology.

More researchers also found that well siblings did not look seriously disturbed, but the theories of pathological families still held firm. These notions had risen out of earlier writings such as Haley's (1969) theory that double-bind communication within the family caused schizophrenia. Lidz et al. (1963) had seen the whole family as ill. To reconcile the idea of such sick families with the simultaneous fact of well siblings, others now offered the hypothesis that the well siblings had managed to detach from the family and escape its effects, whereas the schizophrenic sibling had not. This sibling was distinct in some way: was the only boy or only girl in the family, was more sickly, more passive, or more agressive; or had more attention from the parents. As Kadushin (1963) observed while writing about diagnostic reports, this theory is an "Aunt Fanny" description: a statement that is diagnostically valid for the client but would be equally as true of his—or anybody's—"Aunt Fanny."

The paper "Schizophrenic Patients and Their Siblings" (Lidz et al., 1963) said that all schizophrenic people grow up in seriously disturbed homes. The authors studied twenty-four siblings and concluded that only five of six were "making reasonably adequate adjustments." The rest, they said, were suffering from "a variety of clinical neuroses." The paper did not define terms, so it is hard to know what the authors meant. The ways they explained pathology are highly speculative, e.g., that the parents' struggle with incestuous and homosexual tendencies left the ill child unable to resolve his Oedipal problems and gain a secure sexual identity; the ill child was a family scapegoat; or the well sibling was less favored, therefore neglected, and thus spared the toxic effect of the parents.

By the late 1960s, some of this thinking was being questioned. Pollack et al. (1969) wrote that to test both genetic and psychogenic theories about the cause of schizophrenia, it is critical to understand siblings. These authors compared their findings with those of Lidz et al. (1963) and saw differences that "cast doubt upon the environmental hypothesis" (p. 657). Looking at some of the twin studies, they concluded that caution is needed in making interpretations. "In view of the minimal evidence . . . it appears premature to postulate such specific intrafamilial patterns of transmission of pathology as are offered by Lidz et al." (1963, p. 657). They contended that none of the family interactional patterns thought to contribute to pathology had been substantiated by methodologically sound studies.

After reviewing the studies of families of schizophrenic patients, Brown (1966) pointed out that dogmatic claims to knowledge about schizophrenia—whether based on genetic or environmental theories—are likely to hinder progress. He said we do not have the knowledge to explain etiology adequately, and he cautioned that we may also cause more suffering to families who have already suffered a great deal. (In light of this, it is not surprising that very few first-person accounts were written during this period.)

The 1970s literature still speculated about causes of SMI, but siblings now appeared in a more benevolent light (e.g., Hoover & Franz, 1972; Samuels & Chase, 1979). In 1974 the first literature review was done on relatives' reactions to serious mental illness, as opposed to their hypothetical role in causing the illness. This decade also saw siblings beginning to speak up for themselves (Anonymous, 1973; Kreisman & Joy, 1974).

One problem was that some of the research on siblings in the early 1970s lumped together mental illnesses, developmental disabilities, and even physical illnesses. These different disabilities all have their own etiologies and problems, and they affect the ill individual and their siblings differently.

People continued to explain the positive outcomes of many siblings by the theory of "saving rejection." That is, if your parents were disturbed enough to cause your sibling's severe mental illness, you would be lucky to be rejected by your parents. At the same time, the notion that rejecting parents caused schizophrenia (i.e., the "schizophrenegenic mother") was still alive and well. It seemed that parents either caused or prevented serious mental illness by rejecting their children.

In the later 1970s, researchers came up with data to suggest that the severity of disturbances seen in siblings of people with severe mental illness was no greater than in families without SMI offspring. In addition, writers focused more on describing findings rather than speculating about their findings. In "The Well Siblings of Schizophrenics," Samuels and Chase (1979) described fourteen high-functioning siblings they had interviewed. Guilt was a dominant emotion for them, and its intensity related to birth order: younger siblings, particularly same-sexed younger siblings, expressed the most guilt about being free of SMI.

A comparatively small body of literature from professionals has emerged since 1980. Exploring family attitudes toward schizophrenia and child-bearing, Schulz et al. (1982) addressed the ever-present genetic concerns of siblings. Asked what they thought the risk to their offspring would be for developing schizophrenia, all eight siblings in this study consistently overestimated the risk. This did not keep them from wishing to have children, however. At least among these eight individuals, the wish for children overrode genetic fears.

Bank and Kahn (1982) said that all the well siblings they interviewed feared becoming mentally ill. The more they physically resembled the ill brother or sister, the greater their fear. These siblings were all relatively young—under age twenty. (In our twenty interviews, all but four siblings said genetic counseling would have been helpful.)

It was heartening to find Landeen et al. (1992) writing about the "Needs of Well Siblings of Persons with Schizophrenia." They pointed out that siblings have specific needs that differ from those of other family members. In their study of thirty-four siblings, 87 percent wanted information about schizophrenia and 75 percent wanted genetic information.

They ran support and information groups for all the siblings. Their major findings were that the group members liked best the knowledge they had gained and the chance to share experiences with other siblings. All were apprehensive about the great responsibility they would carry after the death of their parents. The authors also said, "It is of note that most respondents had been disappointed with health professionals in relation to their siblings' illness" (p. 268).

LITERATURE BY SIBLINGS

The first literature written by siblings appeared in the 1970s and had a very different slant from that of researchers. The 1973 article "In Defense of the Schizophrenic Family" was by an anonymous psychotherapist who was also a sibling, and who wrote: "I have felt for many years that my lips were sealed" (p. 58). The article talks about how hostile Haley, Szasz, and Laing were toward the families of people with severe mental illness. "Because we all felt so guilty, we were desperately lonely with our own private burdens. No one could comfort anyone else" (p. 58).

The author also talks about hugging his or her sick brother and crying for the loss he or she felt when that brother became ill. A vivid passage portrays everyone in the family trying to protect each other: parents trying to protect all their children, and children trying to protect their parents.

This early sibling literature described professionals keeping families in the dark and leaving them thus completely ill prepared to care for their SMI member after release from the hospital. The experience was terribly frightening for all concerned. Siblings saw the confidentiality issue as anti-family. (This is still a common complaint among family members in the 1990s, according to our interviewees.) Sibling literature blamed professionals in the 1970s as much as professionals had blamed families twenty years earlier.

The siblings who did speak up talked of their pain, loss, and need for help. They also expressed their deep and loving concern for their ill brothers and sisters. "Rarely do therapists make use of our ability to provide a healing touch and simple kindness that can never be purchased from a professional. Well siblings can be allies" (Anonymous, 1973, p. 66).

Since the mid 1980s, more literature has come from siblings than professionals. At the 1989 NAMI convention, Sue Estroff spoke movingly from her unpublished paper "Rights, Roles, and Responsibilities: A Sibling's Perspective" (1989). Her tones of agony, anger, and compassion conveyed even more than the words. Under the heading of "Rights" she wrote: "As a sibling, I have the right to a safe, nourishing, and comfortable family life and home. One that is not dominated entirely by the anguish and chaos within and around my sib," and "I have the right to succeed without feeling guilty. I have the right not to be perfect, and thus to feel anger and sorrow when I see the suffering and damage experienced by my family." Under "Responsibilities," she said:

> It is my responsibility to be there for and with
> my sibling when my parents are gone. To be
> family for him or her . . . to keep open the

> heart of a sister, the open heart of one whose commitment is enduring and unbreakable, though within limits. It is my responsibility to provide that trust and comfort for all of us. My most important responsibility is to see my sib as my sib—to see the person, not the illness. To save a place for my sib to be just my sister or brother, not someone with a diagnosis or a brain disease.

Estroff is both a sibling and a professional researcher, and she expressed eloquently the themes of the 1980s.

Johnson (1988), also both a sibling and a professional, wrote the first book on siblings of people with severe mental illness. *Hidden Victims,* the title, captures her main theme. She wrote her book to help siblings move beyond just coping, to create the delicate balance between caring for self and caring for the sibling with SMI, to "live beyond the disruption that the mental illness has caused" (p. 23).

In describing how siblings sometimes sacrifice their own pleasures to keep their guilt under control, Johnson cautioned: "if you give it all away, there will be nothing left" (p. 57). She wrote about shame, guilt, confusion, fear, sense of responsibility, trying to escape from family chaos, and ever-present genetic fears. Johnson recommended: Mourn your losses, own up to your own feelings, and know and accept your siblings as they are now, not as they were.

Aronowitz (1988) talked about his ill brother's suffering: "I think of his crossed wires, of receptors and neurotransmitters, deficits and surpluses, progress and relapse, and I wonder what has happened to my brother" (p. 35). He described holidays, once happy occasions for his family, as emotional torture sessions. He also expressed enormous sadness because he dreams of a future and he knows his brother does not.

Swados' compelling book *The Four of Us* (1991) described the loss, grief, frustration, and pain for the entire family. She also made clear the additional suffering caused by lack of knowledge about mental illness. Her story covered the period from 1960 to 1990 and thus provided the big and changing picture. She described massive ignorance on the part of professionals and family alike, which in turn devastated every member of the family. "The effects of mental illness became a dominating force in our home because no one could face that it existed" (p. 4). In 1989 when her brother finally died, his schizophrenia was still a family secret.

When her brother was found dead on the streets of Manhattan in a most pitiful state, the police did not want Swados to see him. "It seemed ironic that I was never going to be allowed to spend time with my brother. In life or in death" (p. 47). Deveson (1991) described an identical scene that had occurred across the world ten years earlier, in Australia. There, too, the police had not wanted Deveson to view the horrors to which societies allow the mentally ill to fall victim. In both cases, the bodies were emaciated, filthy, and diseased. Like Swados, Deveson needed to see her beloved one more time.

Deveson (1991, p. 84) also writes of her well children:

> Our whole family was like a ship engulfed in a terrible storm. As we were swept from one crises to another, G. and J. must have felt in danger of being overwhelmed. They had to deal with their own paradox of anger and grief. They also had to deal with their anger towards me, and with the indignation they must have felt that the one who was misbehaving was getting all the attention.

Moorman's 1992 book, *My Sister's Keeper,* is a beautifully written account of her long struggle from rejection to acceptance of her sister with SMI. It was only by her mother's grave, months after death, that the ill sister acknowledged how desperately and loyally her mother had tried to help and protect her all of her life. And during this acknowledgment, too late for the long-suffering mother, Moorman knew she would become her sister's keeper.

A striking aspect of the literature coming from siblings is their sensitivity to their ill brothers or sisters, and to their parents, as well as to themselves. Of course, we are only hearing from those siblings who have chosen to write. Since writing often reflects a process of conflict resolution, we may be getting a biased sample from those siblings who have chosen to tell their stories.

Aside from writing books about their experiences, siblings also have formed groups at local and national levels, such as NAMI's Sibling and Adult Children Network. Sharing their experiences and pooling their expertise, brothers and sisters of the SMI have helped each other tremendously and have developed many resources for themselves. One example is the accompanying article, "Sixty Signposts for Siblings and Adult Children" (Dickens, 1990). Such material often helps people feel less alone, offers insight into many different feelings, and helps validate siblings' perceptions of themselves. As such, this list is a fitting conclusion for this section on literature by siblings.

60 Signposts for Siblings & Adult Children

by Rex Dickens, *NAMI Siblings and Adult Children Network*

Siblings and adult children must take care of themselves as they care for their relative who has a mental illness. Here are 60 things to remember:

1. You cannot cure a mental disorder for a family member.
2. Despite your best efforts, symptoms may get worse, or they may improve.
3. If you feel inordinate resentment, you are giving too much.
4. It is as hard for the [SMI] individual to accept the disorder as it is for other family members.
5. Disorder acceptance by all concerned may be helpful, but not necessary.

6. A delusion is not amenable to reason, therefore needs no discussion.
7. You may learn something about yourself as you learn about a family member's mental disorder.
8. Separate the person from the disorder.
9. Separate medication side effects from the disorder and the person.
10. It is not okay for you to be neglected. You have emotional needs and wants also.
11. Your chances [of developing an SMI] as a sibling or adult child (1st order) are 10 to 14%. If you are past 30, they are negligible for schizophrenia.
12. Your children's chances (2nd order) are approximately 2 to 4%, compared to the general population of 1%.
13. The illness of a family member is nothing to be ashamed of. The reality is that you may encounter stigma from an apprehensive public.
14. No one is to blame.
15. Don't forget your sense of humor.
16. It may be necessary to renegotiate your emotional relationship.
17. It may be necessary to revise your expectations.
18. Success for each individual may be different.
19. Acknowledge the remarkable courage your family member may show in dealing with a mental disorder.
20. Your family member is entitled to his own life journey, as you are.
21. Survival-oriented response is often to shut down your emotional life; resist this.
22. Inability to talk about your feelings may leave you stuck or "frozen."
23. The family relationships may be in disarray in the confusion around the mental disorder.
24. Generally, those closest in sibling order and gender become emotionally enmeshed while those further out become estranged.
25. Grief issues for siblings are about what you had and lost; for adult children, about what you never had.

26. After denial, sadness, and anger comes acceptance. The addition of understanding yields compassion.
27. The mental illnesses, like other diseases, are a part of the varied fabric of life.
28. Shed neurotic suffering and embrace real suffering.
29. The mental illnesses are not on a continuum with mental health.
30. It is absurd to believe you may correct a physical illness such as diabetes, the schizophrenias, or manic-depression with talk, although addressing social complications may be helpful.
31. Symptomology may change over time while the underlying disorder remains.
32. The disorder may be periodic, with times of improvement and deterioration, independent of your hopes or actions.
33. You should request the diagnosis and its explanation from professionals.
34. Schizophrenia may be a class of disorders rather than homogeneous.
35. Identical diagnosis does not mean identical etiology (cause).
36. Strange behavior is a symptom of the disorder. Don't take it personally.
37. You have a right to assure your personal safety.
38. Don't shoulder the whole responsibility for your mentally disordered relative yourself.
39. You are not a paid professional caseworker. Work with them about your concerns. Your role is to be a sibling or child of (not a parent or caseworker); maintain your role.
40. Mental health professionals, family members, and the disordered person all have ups and downs when dealing with a mental disorder.
41. Forgive yourself and others for mistakes made.
42. Mental health professionals have varied degrees of competence.
43. If you can't care for yourself, then you can't care for another.
44. You may eventually forgive your family member for having a mental disorder.

45. The needs of the ill person do not necessarily always come first.

46. It is important to have boundaries and to set clear limits.

47. Most modern researchers favor a genetic, biochemical (perhaps interuteral), or viral basis. Each individual case may be one, a combination, or none of the above. Genetic predisposition may result from a varied single gene or a combination. Psychoanalytic and family interaction theories are now largely discounted. Stress theories have no supporting data, although once manifest, the disorders are stress-sensitive. Evidence does not support drug abuse theories.

48. Learn about the mental disorders: *Surviving Schizophrenia: A Family Manual* by E.F. Torrey, MD, 1988; *Overcoming Depression* (for family members also) by Dr. D. and J. Papolos, revised 1992.

49. Excerpt from *Surviving Schizophrenia: A Family Manual* by E. Fuller Torrey, MD: "Schizophrenia randomly selects personality types, and families should remember that persons who were lazy, manipulative, or narcissistic before they got sick are likely to remain so as schizophrenic.

"As a general rule, I believe that most persons with schizophrenia do better living somewhere other than home. If a person lives at home, two things are essential—solitude and structure.

"In general, treat the ill family member with dignity as a person, albeit with a brain disease.

"Make communication brief, concise, and unambiguous."

50. It may be therapeutic to help others if you cannot help your family member.

51. Recognizing that a person has limited capabilities should not mean that you expect nothing of them.

52. Don't be afraid to ask your family member if he is thinking about hurting himself. A suicide rate of approximately 10% is based on real people.

53. Mental disorders affect more than the afflicted.

54. Your conflicted relationship may spill over into your relationships with others. You may unconsciously reenact the conflicted relationship.

55. It is natural to experience a cauldron of emotions such as grief, guilt, fear, anger, sadness, hurt, confusion, etc. You, not the ill member, are responsible for your own feelings.
56. Eventually you may see the silver lining in the storm clouds: increased awareness, sensitivity, receptivity, compassion, maturity and become less judgmental, self-centered.
57. Allow family members to maintain denial if they need it. Seek out others.
58. You are not alone. Sharing your thoughts and feelings with others in a sibling/adult support group has been helpful and enlightening for many.
59. The mental disorder of a family member is an emotional trauma. You may pay an emotional price if you do not receive help and support.
60. Siblings and Adult Network material includes:
    Background Information and Articles
    Booklet, 1989 ($5.00); Annotated Book, Audio, and
        Video Lists, 1989 ($3.00);
    "The Bond" quarterly Network newsletter ($10.00
        annually).
    Available from NAMI, 200 North Glebe Road, Suite 1501, Arlington, VA 22203-3754.

Clinical Implications

Given what siblings are saying, both in their writings and as reported from many sibling support groups around the country, the clinical implications seem quite straightforward. When there is mental illness in the family, siblings ought to have the choice to be included in the treatment and caring plans, regardless of age. The implication here is not to offer siblings treatment, but rather to invite them to be included in understanding what is happening to their ill brother or sister, their family, and themselves.

Often the ill member takes up so much time and energy that the well siblings feel lost in the shuffle. To be heard is to be validated. Siblings need to understand that their many strong feelings are normal, not bad or sinful. As with parents and other family members, the process of confusion, denial, and searching for answers about SMI is very lengthy, so siblings need inclusion throughout.

Parents often express frustration and guilt when their well children do not want to discuss SMI with them. It is understandable that children do not want to talk with their parents about such a volatile, painful subject. People process things at their own speed and in their own way. That chidlren do not talk with their parents does not necessarily mean they are not working through things. We need to give each other room and patience (which is hard to do when we are feeling anxious and unhappy).

Written information is especially useful for older children and adolescents—particularly in the area of genetics, since siblings worry about carrying or inheriting the illness. The odds are usually much better than their fears. The genetic background for each family is different. For many families, missing data about past generations and extended family makes it hard to know the possibilities. Still, information and (if people are willing) open discussion on the topic are better than hidden fears.

Another topic of concern, especially for older siblings, is what roles they will take as caregivers after their parents die. No easy answers exist, again, but communication and considering options are better than silence. Planning about the future can comfort people with mental illnesses, their parents, and their siblings. It also generates valuable information for professional providers.

Professionals have overwhelming caseloads and cannot ever give patients all the attention they need. Now I am suggesting that professionals also include siblings. In the long run, however, it may save time and energy, as a well-informed, included sibling may prove to be a big asset for all concerned.

Checklist

Here is a list, by no means definitive, of things to consider when working with siblings. Needless to say, these suggestions need to be modified according to the age and circumstances of each individual.

1. Does the well sibling understand the diagnosis of the ill brother or sister? The nature of the illness? The unpredictability of its course?
2. What does the sibling understand about the causes of the illness?
3. What questions does the sibling have? Where will he or she feel free to turn with future questions? Can you make articles or books available? The younger the sibling, the more you need to follow up.
4. How is this person fitting into the family? Are enough of his or her own needs met, e.g., are the parents providing encouragement and concern about school work, social life, and future plans? If you are working with adult siblings no longer living at home, how do they envision their futures in terms of responsibility toward their ill sibling?
5. What is the quality of this sibling's relationship to the SMI sibling? How comfortable or uneasy does this sibling feel in the relationship? Is the ill sibling younger or older? What is the significance for this sibling in seeing an older or younger sibling suffer?
6. Is this sibling worried about the rest of the family? Does this one try to hold the family together? Wish to just get away from the family?
7. What, if any, genetic concerns does this sibling have?
8. How does the size of the family affect this sibling? Are there other well siblings? If so, how do they relate with this one?
9. Is this sibling interested in knowing about the Siblings Network within NAMI or in the local community?

Whole books could be—and have been—written on siblings (see Johnson's *Hidden Victims,* 1988; and Dickens & Marsh, *Anguished Voices,* 1994). This preceding list simply reminds us of the manifold and complex issues they face.

References

Anonymous (1973). In I. R. DeRoo, In defense of the schizophrenic family: An autobiographical account. Source of this article is unknown.

Arnowitz, P. (1988, Jan. 24). A brother's dreams. *New York Times Magazine, 35.*

Bank, S. P., & Kahn, M. D. (1982). The embroiled family: 'Well' and 'disturbed' siblings. In S. P. Bank & M. D. Kahn (Eds.), *The sibling bond* (pp. 232–270). New York: Basic Books.

Brown, G., Bone, M., Dalison, B., & Wing, J. (1966). *Schizophrenia and social care.* London: Oxford University Press.

Carlisle, W. (1984). *Siblings of the mentally ill.* Saratoga, CA: R & E Publishers.

Chastain, H. (1990). William Tell. *Rainbow Wind, 323.*

Day, J., & Kwitkowska, H. (1962). The psychiatric patient and his 'well' sibling: A comparison through their art productions. *Bulletin of Art Therapy, 1,* 51–66.

Deveson, A. (1991). *Tell me I'm here.* Australia: Penguin Books.

Dickens, R. (1990, Jan./Feb.). Sixty signposts for siblings and adult children. *NAMI Advocate, 14*(1).

Dickens, R., & Marsh, D. (Eds.)(1994). *Anguished voices: Siblings and adult children of persons with psychiatric disabilities, Vol. 2,* No. 1. Boston: Center for Psychiatric Rehabilitation, Boston University.

Estroff, S. (1989). Rights, roles and responsibilities: A sibling's perspective. Paper presented at a meeting of the National Alliance for the Mentally Ill, Cincinnati, OH.

Felt, H. (1986). *What about me?* Videocassette (VHS) available from New Dimensions Films (85803 Lorane Highway, Eugene, OR 97405).

Hoover, C. F., & Franz, J. D. (1972). Siblings in the families of schizophrenics. *Archives of General Psychiatry, 26,* 334–342.

Johnson, J. T. (1988). *Hidden victims: An eight-stage healing process for families and friends of the mentally ill.* New York: Doubleday.

Kadushin, A. (1963). Diagnosis and evaluation for (almost) all occasions. *Social Work, 8*(1): 12–19.

Landeen, J., Whelton, C., Dermer, S., Cardamone, J., Monroe-Blum, H., & Thornton, J. (1992). Needs of well siblings of persons with schizophrenia. *Hospital and Community Psychiatry, 43*(3), 266–269.

Lefley, H. (1987). Research directions for a new conceptualization of families. In H. Lefley & D. Johnson (Eds.), *Families as allies in treatment of the mentally ill* (pp. 127–162). Washington, DC: American Psychiatric Association Press.

Lidz, T., Fleck, S., Alanen, Y. O., & Cornelison, A. (1963). Schizophrenic patients and their siblings. *Psychiatry, 26,* 1–18.

Moorman, M. (1992). *My sister's keeper: Learning to cope with a sibling's mental illness.* New York: Norton.

Newman, G. (1966). Younger brothers of schizophrenics. *Psychiatry, 29,* 146–151.

Pollack, M., Woerner, M. G., Goldberg, P., & Klein, D. F. (1969). Siblings of schizophrenic and nonschizophrenic psychiatric patients. *Archives of General Psychiatry, 20,* 652–658.

Samuels, L., & Chase, L. (1979). The well siblings of schizophrenics. *American Journal of Family Therapy, 7,* 24–35.

Schulz, P. M., Schulz, S. C., Dibble, E., Targum, S. D., van Kammen, D. P., & Gerson, E. S. (1982). Patient and family attitudes about schizophrenia: Implications for genetic counseling. *Schizophrenia Bulletin, 9*(3), 504–513.

Sturges, J. S. (1977). Talking with children about mental illness. *Social Casework, 59,* 530–536.

Swados, E. (1991a). *The four of us.* New York: Farrar, Strauss & Giroux.

Swados, E. (1991b, Aug. 18). The story of a street person: Remembering my brother. *New York Times Magazine,* pp. 16–18, 44–46.

Terkelson, K. G. The meaning of mental illness to the family. In A. Hatfield & H. P. Lefley (Eds.), *Families of the mentally* ill: Coping and adaptation (pp. 128–142). New York: Guilford.

Titelman, D. (1991). Grief, guilt, and identification in siblings of schizophrenic individuals. *The Menninger Letter, 55*(1), 72–84.

IV

S P O U S E S :

The No-Casserole Illness

> You couldn't conceive of a situation in which a relative wouldn't call you if your wife had severe diabetes. But if it's mental illness, forget it. No calls, no casseroles, nothing.
>
> —Carol Grogan (1991)

As with all other family members, the ripple effects of SMI on spouses are grim. This chapter reviews the tiny amount of literature that exists on spouses of people with SMI and then looks at what our twenty well spouses had to say in their interviews. I end with a few clinical implications.

Literature Review

Literature written specifically about or for spouses of SMI people is almost nonexistent. Spousal desire to receive information about SMI and how to cope with it was documented long ago, in 1955 (Clausen & Yarrow; Deasy & Quinn), but nothing was ever done about it. Data about spouses has to be teased out of other literature. Judging from the occasional newsletter or pamphlet written by spouses, and from what our interviewees told us, more studies in this area are sorely needed.

The draft of a paper on spouse support groups (Mannion et al., 1993) reported that 94 percent of 36 well spouses dropped out of a general psychoeducational support group. Obviously, their needs were not being met in groups dominated by parents of children with SMI. A task force then formed to develop a program for spouses. This task force pointed out that parents and spouses have very real differences in their concerns about the future. For instance, parents worry about who will look after their ill child when they die; spouses are more concerned about staying in or getting out of a marriage.

Judge (1993) pointed out that an accepted norm in our culture is for an adult child to live outside the family home. "But unlike the parental relationships, the spousal relationship usually requires physical proximity for its maintenance." Thus, options for spouses of the severely mentally ill are even more constricted than for all other family members.

LITERATURE FROM SPOUSES

The first official spouse support group formed only in 1988. This group, the Well Spouse Foundation (WSF) of San Diego, defined itself as the "well husbands and wives of the mentally ill" and stated that "there are at least 7–9 million of us in the U.S. alone" (1992). By January 1992, fifty such groups had formed. These support groups advocate for change in insurance coverage; educate people, including professionals; and form a national network offering emotional support for "our unusually hidden role" (WSF, 1992). The San Diego WSF brochure states that a well spouse faces emotional and financial loss, a double work load, daily anxiety and stress, loss of pleasure, an overload of responsibility, and single parenting—sometimes for forty years or more.

Carol Grogan, past president of the Dane County AMI of Wisconsin and long-time advocate for developing spouse support groups, tells me she has gotten requests for information from spouse support groups all over the country. Most spouses are busy with full-time jobs and full-time caregiving, she says, so it has been difficult finding people who have time to devote to developing a national organization.

In a 1992 AMI newsletter, Grogan wrote: "Few of our extended families understand the illnesses we live with. After years of stress, many of us have gone on antidepressants as well." In an earlier newsletter (1990), she had stated: "We have waited too long for the world to bring in casseroles and cookies. Other peole who have 'normal' illnesses in their families get neighborhood sympathy, support from their church, and food to eat while an ill spouse is in the hospital. Bring on the food!"

A few poignant comments from other spouse support newsletters mention spouses' frustration with professionals. The most common complaints are: ignorance on the part of professionals, hiding behind confidentiality and not giving the well spouse information or counsel, and not helping well spouses work the legal system on behalf of either themselves or their ill spouses.

Lawyers need to understand SMI, well spouses say, and not get fooled by the SMI spouse. An example is understanding the wild spending spree of someone experiencing a manic episode. In that case, the spree is a symptom of illness—not a mere aberration—and the spouse who is trying to control the damage is not a greedy human being but someone seeking help before the family goes bankrupt. Lawyers too often see the well spouse as the enemy rather than as the partner desperately trying to cope. (This stance is reminiscent of what parents of SMI children went through for decades, and sometimes still do.)

Complaints from spouses frequently indicate their feelings about not being understood. Clergy need to understand what SMI is. Patience and prayer are no substitute for medications and other treatments. Family doctors need to do more than talk about stress reduction and prescribe tranquilizers. They need to recognize SMI and know when to make an appropriate referral to a competent psychiatrist. And psychiatrists, too, need to know about

SMI and not make statements such as: "Let's try life without medications." Well spouses complained the most about psychiatrists not
including them, not listening to their concerns, and "hiding behind
the confidentiality issue."

Of support groups, Grogan (1992) wrote: "We all find
relief . . . lots of laughter. We share clippings, books, suggestions,
and 'doctor' stories. Our time together is precious, funny and sad."
Highlighting what well spouses are up against, she also recalled:
"The first time we met, we all lied to our spouses about our desti-
nation." Well spouses deal with double workloads, reduced social
contacts, and the prejudices and ignorance of society ("Some
members still get their support-group mail at a post office box,"
Grogan mentioned). For some, these stresses are ameliorated by
attending support groups; but groups are not available in everyone's location.

The Progressive magazine published an article on
"Coping with a Spouse's Mental Illness" (Rockstead, 1990), which
echoed many of the same sentiments, including: "We are angry
people . . . just asking for understanding for our fears and feelings.
Until I came here [AMI], there was nobody who understood." Many
professionals avoid contact with the spouses and children of their
patients, and this restricts what professionals know. It is the family
who really lives with and sees behavioral changes on a daily basis.
Still, most doctors do not welcome relatives' input. So families
lament that "There has to be a way to get treatment before absolute
crises and probably total humiliation occurs." This article ends
with a quote from a well spouse: "We're on the battle line . . . the
politics of law and the politics of medicine make us fight"
(p. 15).

LITERATURE FROM PROFESSIONALS

Bernheim, Lewine, and Beale's (1982) excellent book,
The Caring Family: Living with Chronic Mental Illness, has a
chapter that deals with the emotional and physical disruption that
SMI usually produces between a couple. "The overall consequence

[for the well spouse] is to make you feel as if you were no longer married to the person you had originally known" (p. 167).

The mentally ill partner is usually too self-involved to have energy left for others, so the well spouse faces tremendous emotional loss. The inability to share in small talk or daily events is painful. The emotional silence of an ill spouse means that the other receives little or no assurance about being important, valued, or loved. Worse yet, the ill partner may vehemently deride the well spouse for years.

Spouses in such a marriage are no longer equals. Sharing household duties may no longer work, leaving the well spouse with fatigue, anger, and resentment. As the well spouse takes on the responsibility of being primary wage-earner, financial insecurities may arise or increase. In many cases, the well spouse also takes over most of the parenting. Both parents may resent this, and no one outside the household may understand or support the arrangement.

Social isolation is a common problem. Friends and family may drop away. "Physically, emotionally, and psychologically you will find yourselves torn between the need to care for your spouse and your own need to depend on someone and be cared for" (Bernheim et al., 1982, p. 170). If social plans are made at all, they often have to be cancelled when that week's or that day's symptoms threaten to lead to additional embarrassment or stress.

Sexuality is adversely affected. The ill spouse may be less considerate or may lose interest altogether when depression hits. Psychotropic medications produce erectile difficulties for men. A manic spouse may make excessive demands. Sometimes a couple's sex life becomes just one more problem area.

If children live at home, the well spouse may be involved in a tricky balancing act. The desire to protect children from pain and inconsistencies may temper the desire to foster a respect for and a relationship with the ill parent. So much, of course, depends on the ages and personalities of the children, their pre-SMI relationship with their parents, and the degree of disability from the illness.

Other couples may grapple with the issue of whether to risk having any children. Can they cope? What are the genetic risks involved?

Bernheim et al. (1982) also point out that "A spouse's recovery can be just as traumatic for the marital relationship as the initial illness" (p. 173). First, the well partner accommodates and makes adjustments to the illness; then he or she has to readjust once again. When will the other shoe drop? Thoughts of separation and divorce are very common, mostly by the ill partner, who longs for emotional relief and cannot believe that his or her pain comes from within. For the well spouse, on the other hand, "Living with a stranger who drains your emotional and financial resources can be far worse than living with no one at all" (p. 175). As common as these thoughts may be, however, the notion of dissolving a marriage can by scary and guilt-provoking.

Hooley (1987) wrote a fascinating article about *expressed emotion* (EE) in families of the SMI. His research indicated that high levels of criticism, emotional overinvolvement, and self-sacrificing on the part of the well spouse correlate with relapse in the ill spouse. As with similar findings between SMI adult children and their parents, it is not clear which came first, the chicken or the egg. That is, does high EE cause relapse, or does the worsening condition of the SMI person create high EE in the family? In our interviews, for instance, one well spouse's reaction to the high EE concept was "Hogwash! If one damned thing doesn't cause the boil-over, another will. It can be ten different uncontrollable events, different each time: weather, finances, a call from a friend, physical illness—you never know what will set them off." While we don't know which comes first, the clinical implication is that it is helpful to minimize these negative expressions.

A particularly interesting finding in Hooley's research is that marital satisfaction relates to the symptom profile. When SMI spouses have predominantly positive symptoms (e.g., hallucinations or delusions), their partners are significantly happier with their marriages than those married to patients with predominantly negative symptoms (e.g., depression or lack of interest). Since people with positive symptoms usually have much poorer levels of overall functioning, the implication here is that the passivity and withdrawal of negative symptoms are even harder to live with than the disruption caused by florid positive symptoms. (There is a similar finding for spouses of Alzheimer's Disease victims. Many spouses find the depression of Alzheimer's harder to live with than the acting-out symptoms.) Some spouses we interviewed strongly disagree with this finding, however.

In their book on depression, De Paulo and Ablow (1989) wrote: "The ripples of pain touch family members and friends who become, in some way, co-victims" (p. 45). A spouse described her husband's illness, which ultimately ended in suicide. "Now I realize Chicken Little was right—the sky can fall in" (p. 49). Some spouses live in constant fear of suicide.

McElroy and McElroy (1993) wrote about the harm done to family members by the confidentiality issue: "This lack of disclosure by mental health professionals is often viewed as an insensitive disregard for the legitimate concern of families. The lack of critical information can elevate a health crisis to a catastrophic disaster." Indeed, professionals do not keep information away from families in any other medical situation. Pediatricians, coronary specialists, and trauma centers share information with parents, spouses, and family. That professionals have singled out mental illness as an exception indicates a still strong belief that the family is somehow toxic and responsible.

Literature from both professionals and well spouses draws a grim picture of suffering. The spouse with SMI undoubtedly suffers the most, but we need to remember that the well spouse also exists, suffers a great deal, and needs attention.

The Interviews

Our interviewees were all white, from the Midwest (with one exception), and ranged in age from thirty-three to sixty-five. Some came from big cities and some from rural areas, and their educational level ranged from two years of high school through doctoral programs. We were more struck by the similarities among our findings than the differences. Coping with a mentally ill spouse seemed to be an educational and socioeconomic leveler.

The one question that evoked the same response from all of our interviewees was: "Do you have any genetic fears for your children?" The answer was a loud, resounding yes. In a few families, mental illnesses had already shown up in the children or in other relatives, and in all families the worry was ever-present.

The question that met with the highest degree of variability was: "What kind of supports have there been for you?" We sorted the responses into three categories: family, friends, and professionals. Based on our twenty interviews, the only conclusion we can draw about family support is that everything exists, from "absolutely no support" to "both our families have been very supportive." We also found, not surprisingly, that family support evolved and changed over time. Some of the common responses were:

"My parents were good, his were not."
"They just don't understand."
"I wish I could spare the children."
"They advised me to just leave him."
"We didn't turn to the family. They are sympathetic, but not much involved."
"His family thought for twenty-five years that I caused the illness, and my family said it was because I was too capable."

In contrast to the variability we found in family support, we found consistency in the responses about friends. Unfortunately, these spouses reported social isolation and little support from friends. With the exception of one person, interviewees said that friends had dropped away because of their mentally ill spouse. Typical responses were:

"I have very few friends left."
"Only the AMI support group understands."
"People do not want to be involved."
"It has totally redefined relationships."

"It's an amazing degree of isolation."
"They tell you, 'Get on with your life.'"
"I monitor what I say to people, so I don't lose friends."

One person who led a counterculture lifestyle said that friends were very helpful, took the couple in, and encouraged them to get help.

Answers about help from professionals fell into an either/or category. Either they ignored well spouses or they blamed them. Our respondents had very strong feelings about this. While our sample is very small, it mirrors what families have been saying about professionals for the past fifteen years or so (e.g., Hatfield, 1979; Wasow, 1982; Bernheim et al., 1982; Torrey, 1983; Lefley, 1987). In fact, these spousal complaints sound the same as parental complaints, as in:

"They see us as the enemy."
"We are never told anything."
"Hiding behind the confidentiality issue—they never tell me what is going on."

In our sample, the greatest complaint (fifteen out of twenty) was about the confidentiality issue: spouses said their mates' doctors and counselors were giving no guidance aobut how to deal with the SMI mate. None of our interviewees had even learned about AMI from professionals.

Another big problem for spouses occurs because of the relatively high staff turnover in the mental health system. People tire of telling their stories over and over again, and they become discouraged by both the similarities and differences in treatment modalities. If a new therapist uses the same approach, for instance, a spouse may think, "But it never works." If the new therapist suggests an altogether different approach, the spouse may feel suspicious.

One spouse, only four years into his wife's illness, told us: "I've had contact with eighteen different professionals since all this started, and I don't know if I can take any more. I am just appalled at some of their incompetencies and at the experiences we have had." He specified: "After her second full-blown manic episode, the new psychologist wanted to explore our childhoods. The next doctor said: 'Here's your prescription. I'll see you in three months.'" This litany was typical of our respondents, and it is terribly important that professionals understand such experiences.

Throughout this book, examples illustrate how professionals often put family members in a double-bind, no-win situation. That is, if family members want to know what is happening in treatment, the clinician may see their questions as encroaching on the limits set out by confidentiality laws. If family members say nothing, on the other hand, the clinician may perceive them as uncaring. Many families end up immobilized, not knowing in which direction to move. In the end, everyone loses.

Well-meaning professionals can also be put in no-win situations. They are apt to become symbols of frustration, pain, and repeated failure in the eyes of both the patients and their spouses. Conversely, unhappy patients and spouses can become symbols of frustration to professionals who can neither cure nor alleviate the suffering. Most health care professionals, after all, have chosen their fields because they want to cure and to help. Frustration runs high on all sides when there are no cures or easy answers. The true culprits here are the diseases.

Another difficulty mentioned frequently by spouses was negotiating the mental health and legal systems. The bureaucracy, regulations, and paperwork are often experienced as insurmountable. When involuntary medication or hospitalization is at issue, the legal system more often than not obstructs the well spouse from enlisting desperately needed help. Again, of course, these system negotiations are often almost as frustrating for professionals as for spouses (and all family members).

The spouses we interviewed were quick to criticize, and just as quick to express deep gratitude toward those professionals who had truly understood their pain and had advocated on their behalf. Included among the positive reports were: AMI support groups, individual professionals who were exceptionally helpful, a community support program, an excellent police department, and various books. One woman reported a particularly touching development in a small rural community, where a guidance counselor had asked if she would help teach eigth-graders about mental illness. This woman did, saying it had turned out very well for all concerned.

Two of our interview questions received almost twenty different answers. We asked: "How has your spouse's illness influenced your development as an adult?" and "How do you envision your future?" The one common denominator in all responses was that mental illness had deeply influenced each respondent's adult development and vision of the future. But what that development was and how people perceived the future varied a lot.

Even in our small sample, we saw the whole range—from strongly negative to strongly positive—and it was common to see both reactions in the same person.

> "It has made me stronger, but it brought the worst out in me, too."
> "It shook my self-confidence, and I've lost faith in friends, but now I'm less judgmental, and I've developed my own talents."
> "It has both bolstered and crippled me."

A central theme was: "Things will never go back to where they were before." This resounds to a theme in Flanigan's 1992 book, *Forgiving the Unforgivable*. Part of the process she describes is accepting the fact that things can never be the same again after a terrible personal injury. Rereading the interview transcripts of these spouses, I was struck, like Flanigan, by "the ability of human beings to forgive the unforgivable . . . it is a testament to all that is right about our species" (p. 11).

Envisioning the future ran the gamut from "Maybe he'll die and I'll get a second chance" to "I will not let this be a burden in my life." Most people felt sad and discouraged, however, especially if they had decided to stay in the marriage.

Many spouses struggled to keep their families together, though the mental illnesses ripped them apart. They fell into the category of what Lefley (1987) called "supercopers." Several sentences from the interviews stand out as especially poignant: "I feel such great sorrow towards my wife of twenty-five years. The person I knew died in 1985. I try to grieve, but it's complicated by the body that keeps reappearing. It looks like her, but it's not."

Another man said: "You go on automatic pilot and just live from day to day," and "I'm so afraid of the unknown." A wife described her life as "a terror, always waiting for a catastrophe." One emotion that cropped up repeatedly (as it did among all five categories of relatives we interviewed) was self-blame. "I kept thinking if I just tried hard enough, was careful enough, planned well enough—that it was probably my fault."

Many well spouses felt abandoned by their friends: "You stop people cold when you talk about mental illness" and "When friends ask if I'm okay, I lie and say, 'I'm fine.'" Perhaps it is unfair to assume that friends do not want to deal with mental illness. Could part of the responsibility lie with the fact that our culture's prejudices keep spouses "in the closet"? Perhaps this will change in the future, as the public learns more about SMI.

People suffering with mental illnesses seldom have energy left over to care for others. The well spouse does not feel cared for or looked after by the SMI partner. Several spouses mentioned unhappiness over their sex lives. Some of the women said that they felt like mothers to their husbands. One spouse tried hard to keep his three teenage children involved with their mother, but they pointed out to him: "There's no use, Mom doesn't care." Another spouse commented: "I've been a single parent for twenty-six years and no one knows it."

All our respondents said they frequently felt depressed, tired, frustrated, and lonely in their marriages. People talked at length about their sadness and guilt over the times they had (in their opinion) behaved poorly towards their ill spouse. "I felt numb. I tried to reason. She just wouldn't listen. I was desperate. I couldn't work because I had to watch her. We had no money. Out of desperation, I just hauled off and hit her and screamed, 'You're wrecking my life.' I'm just haunted by that memory." Six years after getting divorced from a spouse: "I'm still in love with her, and that's very confusing. I can't get over having abandoned her."

These spouses' random and piecemeal education about SMI is striking. Some learned about SMI entirely on their own, through books; some learned from AMI; others got bits and pieces of information from professionals *when they asked for it*; and some still did not know very much. Knowledge about SMI, treatments, and management skills does not eliminate the agony of seeing a loved one suffer. It will not cure SMI, and it will not create a satisfactory marriage. But it does ameliorate some of the fear, make expectations more realistic, lessen the shame, and minimize not knowing what to do. At best, knowledge can comfort, help people cope more effectively, and even encourage spouses to come out of the closet and make friends for themselves. It can also help spouses understand the grieving process. To educate, inform, and support the well spouse is to help the entire family and the person with SMI.

Clinical Implications

A thorough, ongoing, and compassionate education about SMI, treatments, and community resources appears to be the number one need of spouses with partners who are suffering from mental illness. To do less is to compound an already very difficult situation with unnecessary additional suffering.

Carol Grogan, facilitator for the AMI Spouse Support Group in Dane County, Wisconsin, also gave me the following suggestions for professionals who work with people with mental illness and their spouses. This list was generated by the Spouse Support Group in February 1994.

1. We want you to know that, despite what may be expressions of anger and hostility, we care deeply about our ill family member, and feel as much a desire to get involved in the treatment as we would if he/she were suffering from cancer, a kidney problem, or heart disease. Above all, we want to

have access to you and for you to have access to us and listen
to us. In return, we hope to exercise great care and honesty
in our contacts with you.

2. We want you to help educate us regarding the illness, to let
us know what we can expect regarding behavior patterns, to
explain common characteristics such as the anger often
directed at a spouse and the distortion of events and perspective; to give us information about the diagnosis, medications, and treatment plan; and to direct us to materials we
can read on our own.

3. We want you to view us as a resource and an important
member of the treatment team. We hope you recognize that,
given our close contact with the patient, we may have extensive observations and information regarding behavior
that we feel is of vital importance to you in your diagnosis
and in enabling you to make effective use of the limited time
you can devote to the patient. We may be able to alert you to
some direct questions to ask to more quickly provide our
partner with help that might prevent an oncoming crisis.

4. We may need your support over a period of many years, so
we will need plenty of notice and transitional help if you
change insurance groups, move, or plan to retire in the
foreseeable future.

5. Our situation may require that you, or an alternative who
shares your treatment philosophy, be available in times of
crisis, twenty-four hours a day, especially during holiday
times or particular stress periods. Time is critical when our
spouses begin to deteriorate or escalate. *Hours* of delay at
this point might put our spouses beyond the reach of treatment. Our families' future and our safety are possibly at stake.

6. We need someone who has worked regularly with our family
member's diagnosis. If you have not had success or experience in working with this diagnosis or with couples, please
refer us to someone who does have such experience. Although divorce may eventually be inevitable, we are working now to preserve our marriage and family, and we still
have hope.

7. We urge you to attempt to distinguish, difficult as it may be, between marital discord and the tension that results from living with someone who is mentally ill; to avoid recommendations for traditional marriage counseling and dealing with "relational issues," when the need for treatment is clearly apparent.

8. Most of us are strong advocates of medication, because of the known biochemical causes of serious, long-term mental illness. We hope you use regular talk therapy to encourage medication compliance, help to further self-understanding of the illness, assist us in monitoring behavior by asking leading questions, listen to and encourage input from family members, and offer assistance in the development of patient responsibility for routine daily living skills and self-care. Please ask regularly if your patient is taking the medication as prescribed, and if it is causing any problems that might lead to its discontinuation.

9. We want you to be aware of the chronic worry and stress placed upon all members of families (spouses, live-in partners, children, siblings, and parents) when one member is seriously mentally ill.

10. We think it important that you know about our national family support movement, the Alliance for the Mentally Ill, and our goals of advocacy, support, and education. We welcome calls from new families. Most of us have small libraries and free handouts, as well as support groups. Please refer families to us, and please join our mailing list. You can keep abreast of family issues and might possibly be better able to help our family.

11. We hope you work with our family member to encourage, help seek out, or possibly require additional support services, such as day programs, vocational rehabilitation, or social clubs so that our family member has as full a life as possible and becomes less dependent on us as the only support system. Most of us are covered by private health insurance and are not eligible for publicly funded community support programs.

12.   We hope you will schedule further appointments while the patient is still in your office, rather than relying on the patient's future initiative to call.

13.   Please *consider* the occasional possibility of calling the patient regarding missed appointments and medication issues, if you are aware that things are not going very well.

14.   With *prior patient approval,* we hope you allow us to schedule occasional appointments for our spouse/partner, if he/she feels unable to make the call.

15.   We think it vital that you be willing to allow patient and family to come together occasionally for informational sessions, discussion of problems, or medication management. We hope you might also consider patient–doctor or patient–family contracts regarding behavior issues and medication compliance.

16.   Please discuss with us some possible family alternatives for situations when our family member's behavior deteriorates [e.g., ways to protect the children from their ill parent].

17.   We hope that you carefully screen for any physical/medical causes of the symptoms our spouse is experiencing. If you are not a physician, we remind you that some physical illnesses, such as multiple sclerosis, can cause severe emotional swings. Even dental problems can aggravate an already difficult emotional state. In addition, just because our spouse is mentally ill, we hope you don't ignore physical complaints that are difficult to diagnose. Don't be too quick in assuming that the symptoms are a part of the mental illness.

18.   We urge you to take our fears seriously if our spouses threaten suicide or murder, even if our spouses are patients in a psychiatric institution. We know our spouses well, and we can sense when to take these threats seriously.

References

Beattie, M. (1987). *Codependent no more: How to stop controlling others and start caring for yourself.* New York: Harper & Row.

Bernheim, K. F., Lewine, R. R., & Beale, C. T. (1982). *The caring family: Living with chronic mental illness.* New York: Random House.

Black, C. (1981). *It will never happen to me.* New York: Ballantine Books.

Clausen, J., & Yararow, M. R. (Eds.) 1995). The impact of mental illness on the family. *Journal of Social Issues, 11* (special issue).

Deasy, L. C., & Quinn, O. W. (1955). The wife of the mental patient and the hospital psychiatrist. *Journal of Social Issues, 11,* 49–60.

De Paulo, J. R., & Ablow, K. R. (1989). *How to cope with depression.* New York: McGraw-Hill.

Fadden, G., Bebbington, P., & Kuipers, L. (1987). Caring and its burdens: A study of the spouses of depressed patients. *British Journal of Psychiatry, 151,* 660–667.

Flanigan, B. (1992). *Forgiving the Unforgivable.* New York: Macmillan.

Gibbons, J. S., Horn, S. H., & Powell, J. M. (1984). Schizophrenic patients and their families: A survey in a psychiatric service based on a DGH unit. *British Journal of Psychiatry, 144,* 70–75.

Grogan, G. (1990, April). Untitled article in newsletter from AMI of Dane County (Madison, WI).

Grogan, G. (1992, March 25). Letter for AMI of Dane County. In newsletter from AMI of Dane County (Madison, WI).

Hatfield, A. B. (1979). Help-seeking behavior in families of schizophrenics. *American Journal of Community Psychology, 7,* 563–569.

Hooley, J. M. (1987). The nature and origins of EE. In D. Hahlweg & M. J. Goldstein (Eds.), *Understanding major mental* disorder: The contribution of family interaction research (pp. 176–194). New York: Family Process Press.

Judge, K. (1994). Serving children, siblings and spouses: Understanding the needs of other family members. In H. Lefley & M. Wasow (Eds.), *Helping families cope with mental illness* (pp. 161–194). New York: Harwood Academic Publishers/Gordon & Breach.

Lefley, H. P. (1987). An adaptation framework: Its meaning for research and practice. In A. B. Hatfield & H. P. Lefley (Eds.), *Families of the mentally ill: Coping and adaptation*. New York: Guilford.

Mannion, M. F. T., Mueser, K., & Solomon, P. (1993). Designing psychoeducational services for spouses of persons with SMI. Unpublished article.

McElroy, E., & McElroy, E. M. (1993). Family concerns about confidentiality and SMI: Ethical implications. In H. Lefley & M. Wasow (Eds.), *Helping Families Cope with mental illness* (pp. 195–222). New York: Harwood Academic Publishers/Gordon & Breach.

Rockstead, A. (1990, Sept.). Coping with a spouse's mental illness. *The Progressive,* p. 15.

Smith, M. (1988). *When I say no, I feel guilty.* New York: Bantam.

Strong, M. (1988). *Mainstay: For the well spouses of the chronically ill.* New York: Penguin.

Subby, R. (1987). *Lost in the shuffle: The co-dependent reality.* Pompano Beach, FL: Health Commuications.

Targum, S. D., Dibble, E. D., & Davenport, Y. B. (1981). The family attitudes questionnaire: Patients' and spouses' views of bipolar illness. *Archives of General Psychiatry, 18,* 562–568.

Torrey, E. F. (1983). *Surviving schizophrenia: A family manual.* New York: Harper and Row.

Wasow, M. (1982). *Coping with schizophrenia: A survival manual for parents, relatives, and friends.* Palo Alto, CA: Science and Behavior Books.

The Well Spouse Foundation (1992). Brochure. San Diego, CA: San Diego Alliance for the Mentally Ill.

V

GRANDPARENTS:

The Triple Whammy

Locating grandparents to interview proved difficult. The age of most grandparents of mentally ill grandchildren is high, and today's elderly are probably more reticent regarding family troubles than younger people are. It took two years to find twenty grandparent volunteers. Of them, nineteen were grandmothers; the one grandfather was a retired professor. So we have nothing even resembling a cross sample of grandparents. Still, their words are valuable, and we are grateful for what they gave us. Much more research needs to be done in this area.

The Literature

Literature on aging (e.g., Troll, 1983) reports that children view grandparents as the most significant people in their lives, after their parents. But as of 1993, in the literature on families of the seriously mentally ill, I could find only one page on grandparents (Marsh, 1992). No literature whatsoever exists written by grandparents.

Our very limited findings support what Troll (1983) said about the role of grandparents in the U.S. family. They are the "watchdogs" who step in and help during times of family troubles. This is not the idyllic role of grandparenting that most of us like to envision, but the majority of our interviewees agreed with Troll's watchdog concept.

One interviewee also supported Marsh's (1992) point that little attention has been given to the extended family. Literature on disability suggests both the importance and the complexity of studying this, according to Marsh, "particularly with respect to grandparents. In the case of the disability of a grandchild, for example, grandparents often experience a dual grief as they mourn for the loss of a normal grandchild . . . and [have] feelings of helplessness over a persistent and unresolvable family crisis" (p. 134).

The Interviews

Now to report on the poignant words of the interviewed grandparents. One eighty-six-year-old grandmother said she "always had a sense that something was wrong with [her] granddaughter who has schizophrenia, even when she was an infant." She expressed a "triple whammy": feeling a loss for herself, her own child, and for the grandchild. Most of the grandparents we interviewed expressed this feeling in one way or another.

This woman said she felt very sad, especially when she thinks of the future of her grandchild. When asked what she thought caused her granddaughter's SMI, she said she saw it as a brain disease. Her daughter is a very active member of AMI and has educated her mother about SMI, for which the mother/grandmother expressed appreciation. She also said the tragedy has made her closer to her daughter, and she is very proud of what her daughter is doing in the AMI movement.

Another of our grandparents had a ninth-grade education, was seventy-seven years old, and had very little money. Having little understanding of SMI, she found it very hard to accept her grandson's illness and did a lot of reminiscing about how wonderful he had been before the illness. She also felt, however, that he had been "odd" right from the beginning. When asked how his illness made her feel, she replied: "Very sad. I don't want to talk about it." All of what she said and described led us to believe that she was very kind and loving toward this grandchild. When we asked: "Would you have liked any help or information about your grandson's illness?" she said: "I'm too old now." She truly seemed not to want to know about SMI, and we respected her wish.

In partial contrast was the "over eighty years" grandfather who had a doctorate and was well educated about SMI. Although he was very knowledgeable about SMI, his sadness and pain seemed not surprisingly similar to the previous grandmother. His grandson had committed suicide two years prior to our interview. To the question about how he thought the suicide had affected his son, he replied: "It was catastrophic." How did it affect him? "Continuously and very sadly." He felt that the tragedy of SMI had brought him closer to his son. (Most of our grandparents felt this.) Had any professional ever included him in the treatment process? "No." Was there any help you would have liked? "Friendship."

In selecting materials from our interviews, I found myself pulled toward reporting contrasts. Once I wrote these down, however, similarities seemed more apparent, despite people's divergent backgrounds. We interviewed a sixty-four-year old Afro-American with very little formal education. Without knowing the diagnosis of her grandson (it was schizophrenia), she said he was "very nervous" and that she had always known something was wrong. "He was always on some kind of medication, fell behind in school, and couldn't hold a job." When the mother and stepfather could no longer handle him, in his mid-teens, he came to live with her. "They didn't know how to handle him. I did. I feel so very sorry for him. I do all kinds of things for him. I know him better than anyone else."

When asked what she thought caused his illness—or "nerves," as she put it—she said she thought it was "because of bad experiences with his parents and his girlfriend." She knew nothing about SMI, and she said no professional had ever explained anything to her, even though she stayed involved with her grandson throughout, including visits to the jail and mental hospitals when he was incarcerated.

"How has his illness affected you?"

"Oh, I don't know. I can't talk about it," she replied. "I just want him to get back to the way he used to be. He makes me so sad, but I try not to let it get me down. I'll be here for him as long as I'm living. I hope I can die knowing he is okay." She made this last statement three times during the course of our interview.

Would she like a little information now about her grandson's condition?

"No. We just have to pray that he'll be okay, that's all."

This is the only interview that prompted me to wonder whether education about SMI might be counterproductive. I wondered because this grandmother had faith that her grandson would be better one day. She kept the faith for herself, and she was keeping the faith for him. If she believed his condition was more serious, would she still keep the faith? A disquieting thought, with no answer.

An eighty-one-year-old grandmother seemed the personification of coping through the "it could be worse" modality. She stands out in my mind because hers was one of the worst situations we had come across. Her only child had an SMI, and this child's two children also both suffered with SMIs. The grandmother had a wonderful attitude: "These illnesses are something you can't explain. You want to help, and then you see that it is not really helping. So the best thing that you can do is let them know that you love them no matter what."

This grandmother had had both breasts removed because of cancer. Her reply to "You've been through so much hardship" was: "Oh, it could have been worse." She repeated that sentence often throughout the interview.

When asked what she thought had caused the SMI, she gave answers that implied both nature and nurture, i.e., "The atmosphere you live in, and the troubles in the house. But she didn't get it from my side of the family. I don't know about my husband's background."

"How has this affected you?"

"I've not suffered over it; it could be worse." She ended the interview saying with pride, "They always come to me."

We interviewed a comparatively young (fifty-eight years old) grandmother, highly educated, about her twelve-year-old granddaughter who had already had several hospitalizations for what appears to be severe mental illness. What did she think caused her granddaughter's troubles?" "It is in the family, on both sides, multiple relatives, a heavy loading."

"Do you have hope for her recovery?" we asked.

"There is always that hope. You never give up on a twelve-year-old."

When asked how the child's illness affected the rest of the family, she clearly saw the ripple effects on everyone: herself and her husband; the mother, father, and sibling of the ill child; and the extended family. She felt it had been very hard on all of them, though it had brought her closer to her daughter. She and her husband try to be very supportive.

The theme of guilt was surprisingly strong among our sample of grandparents. People often said: "I should have done more." For those whose grandchild had died, this was especially apparent. "Grandparents occupy a special place in their grandchild's lives, and when they die we feel enormous guilt, sorrow, and helplessness." A very elderly grandmother of six grandchildren said: "His death is in the back of my mind all of the time. You always feel guilty about not having done enough. We know he wanted to come back to us, but we put the demand on him that first he had to promise he would take his meds, and he wouldn't. Then he killed himself. I can't bear to think about his death."

Our interviewees—all of whom were involved with their respective grandchild when she or he became SMI—complained about not being told about the illness by professionals. They wished they had been given a diagnosis, explanations about causes, and information about how to be helpful. The general consensus was that hospital nurses tended to be friendly and kind, and psychiatrists aloof.

Two themes emerged from the question: "How has your grandchild's SMI affected your life?" One theme had to do with life feeling less stable. This is particularly interesting in light of how long these grandparents have lived. Presumably, they have had more experiences in life than any other group of relatives; yet the SMI still looms so large that it makes their lives feel less stable. How sad.

The other theme had to do with effects of increased knowledge about SMI. A typical example of this was: "We never knew anything about SMI; now we do. It's not 'them and us' anymore— it's all of us together."

Four interviews were with foster grandparents, and so technically do not belong in our sample. (We were able to find only 16 biological grandparents in our area.) But one finding was striking. All four foster grandparents had been given genuine help by social services, which they appreciated very much. One dares not draw conclusions from such a tiny sample, but could it be that social services correctly assume that foster grandparents deserve and need some guidance, but incorrectly assume that biological grandparents do not? Other agents for change probably exist who could include helping grandparents, thereby widening the pool of support for families in crises. The American Association for Retired Persons, television stations, community colleges, and the YWCA/YMCA are some examples. Any or all of them could provide grandparents with additional information about mental illnesses.

All our interviewees felt a "triple whammy" of grief, and they were doing all they knew how to help out. Given what Troll's research says about the importance of the grandchild–grandparent relationship, and given that people are living longer today, so that we have many three- and even four-generational families, we need to include grandparents in the treatment process. We need to know more about their needs. Then, as with all other relatives, we may widen the pool of support for all concerned.

Clinical Implications

This chapter is short only because there is no literature about grandparents of people with SMI, from either professionals or grandparents. I hope there will be in the future, as grandparents clearly are affected and play an important role in many cases.

No support groups exist for grandparents that I am aware of, so I am unable to consult with such a group to generate a checklist for clinical implications. Instead, let me emphasize the obvious: always ask clients whether grandparents are alive, and how they are involved with the rest of the family. Find out if they would like to be contacted, either to offer their input or to benefit from yours.

Grandparents enjoy tremendous satisfaction when their children and grandchildren create full lives. This holds deep meaning for grandparents. Having a healthy, competent grandchild can bestow a sense of completion and continuity as well as added affection, both given and received. In sharp contrast, people we interviewed expressed raw pain over the illness of their grandchildren.

So if you have an opportunity to reach out to grandparents and offer whatever information or comfort they can use, do it. In addition to helping them, such involvement may also serve to strengthen the whole family's generational bonds.

References

Marsh, D. (1992). *Families and mental illness: New directions in professional practice.* New York: Praeger.

Troll, L. E. (1983). Grandparents: The family watchdogs. In T. Brubaker (Ed.), *Family relationships in later life* (pp. 63–74). Beverly Hills, CA: Sage.

VI

EXTENDED FAMILY:

"What Is Going On?"

The inclusion of extended family members in this study was inspired by two incidents. One involved a young graduate student who had chosen to major in the study of severe mental illness because of the dominating influence over her family of an uncle with schizophrenia. "Can you imagine," she asked me, "he is my uncle, he lives only forty miles away, and I've never been allowed to see him? What is the terrible secret in our family? I'm not allowed to bring the subject up at home." She wanted to learn more about SMI so she could better understand the family secret and her consequent fears.

The second inspiration involves my own first cousin once removed (who is a second cousin to my son with schizophrenia). To pretest an interview outline, we asked him: "How do you see your relationship to your second cousin in the future?"

"Well, obviously, I will join my cousins in looking after him after his mother dies," he replied.

Maybe it is "obvious" to my lovely cousin, but this potential role may not be apparent to most people in our culture. That a second cousin might be there to help and support, as a matter of course, is important for family members and professionals to know.

Our subsequent study confirmed that many members of the extended family were willing and able to give direct care to their SMI relatives. Others were very supportive of the immediate family without being involved in direct care.

All extended family are not involved or caring. No one can estimate what percentage is, or to what degree. Such variability prevailed among our interviews with five cousins, five aunts, five uncles, three nieces, and two nephews that we can make few generalizations about the extended family. Our respondents made it clear, however, that the whole family is always aware of a relative with SMI. The most commonly voiced question was: "What is going on?"

The Literature

As was the case with grandparents, we found virtually no literature on the relationship between people with SMI and their extended family. Neither relatives nor researchers have published anything specifically devoted to this topic.

One exception was Diane Marsh's excellent book (1992), *Families and Mental Illness: New Directions in Professional Practice*. She did not write about specific extended family categories— aunts, uncles, cousins, nephews, nieces—but she pointed out that various relatives function along a continuum of family support. SMI's impact on extended families has received no attention, she said, although the "reverberations of this unnatural family disaster propagate beyond the immediate family" (pp. 133–134).

The Interviews

In contrast to all other family categories, extended family members had fewer genetic fears. Two cousins stated they had no genetic concerns at all. One man, who had both a cousin and an aunt with schizophrenia, was knowledgeable about severe mental illness and told us he assumed the genetic probabilities in his case were small.

We were struck by the negative power of ignorance. The less people knew about mental illness, the greater their fears. A niece in her twenties said: "I think counseling for all family members is essential. I think a lot of us are afraid we're going to get it. It's like a person with the disease is in the middle of a family circle . . . and the family members are experiencing it, too. When we feel blamed for our relative's illness, we have this terrible amount of guilt to live with. With guilt, you end up blaming the person who is mentally ill, in many ways." This person went on to explain that because so little is known about mental illness, family members got angry at themselves and then took it out on their relative with SMI.

The older our interviewees were, the more they leaned toward believing in "nurture" as a cause of severe mental illness. This is in keeping with the thinking of the era in which they grew up. One cousin blamed his aunt for his cousin's illness: "She was too bossy, unfriendly, and spoiled him." This cousin firmly believed that mental illness was caused by bad parenting. A sixty-four-year-old cousin said: "He was just spoiled. They were too easy on him." An eighty-eight-year-old aunt said: "It's so sad. She just got married too young and had too many children, and her husband was not nice to her." Indeed, these factors may have played a role in her illness; the circumstances described were very grim.

Two uncles from different families were at the opposite end of the continuum. (This certainly keeps us on our toes and away from drawing simplistic conclusions.) One sixty-three-year-old uncle, a health care professional, said: "His illness was caused by bad parenting. My sister didn't know how to raise him. No, I never joined AMI, because they weren't optimistic enough." The other uncle, also middle-aged and a professional health care worker, was the number one support and advocate in the family for the seriously mentally ill person. He helped the family get medication for his nephew, and he took it upon himself to keep the family informed about SMI and treatments. "I'm the fix-it man in the family."

Several extended family members said they had little involvement with their SMI relative and did not want any. Then, in contradiction, they went on to describe quite a bit of family loyalty and involvement. We talked with a sixty-nine-year-old aunt, for example, who had had no contact with her niece while she was growing up, but did now that the girl's mother—this aunt's sister—was dead. "I've had it with the girl. Mental illness is my enemy. I'm not going to get involved." She went on to describe how she invites this niece to all family reunions, Christmas, and Easter dinner. "Oh, and I take her shopping when she wants to go."

Throughout these interviews, a significant factor in family involvement was the personality of the relative with mental illness. If the sick relative was comparatively easy to manage rather than difficult and/or violent, the extended family was more apt to stay involved. This is not surprising, but it may play a bigger role with extended family than with closer relatives who feel more obligation.

A fifty-five-year-old aunt whose sister had died said: "I really don't want anything to do with [my niece], to tell the truth. I am here, and she can call me on the phone, and I'll take her shopping, and I'll defend her as far as I can. But she's awful. It is absolute hell. I am not the least bit afraid of hell, because I have had it. You can't imagine. It is worse than the people with severe mental illness you see in the hospitals, because there is control over them in the hospital. When you have a person with severe mental illness at home, it is so frightening."

Many respondents spoke of both the positive and the negative influences of their mentally ill relatives. A niece says: "I didn't see [my aunt] much as I got older and she got sicker. I feel guilty about that now. But I was scared of her. But now, the more I learn about severe mental illness, the less frightened I am." To the question about her genetic concerns, she responded: "I thought somewhere along the line I'd become receptive to the illness. I thought, 'Uh, oh, here it comes.' You just never know whether or not it is going to happen to you." Toward the end of the interview, this woman spoke of her aunt's positive influence. "It's made me a more sensitive and compassionate person. Granted, I'm not the caregiver who has to be there every day."

It also seems that the mental illness influenced many relatives' philosophy of life. "If there's anything that I've learned from all of this, it's that these people are just as special as the next person. In some ways, I believe God blessed us and gave us this life, and there's a reason for it. I try to find that reason. One life is never more important than another."

A nephew said: "I've changed, just knowing that there are people in the world that are like [my uncle] and that not everyone is perfect. There but for the grace of God go I."

On the topic of how they viewed professional help, extended family members had a wide variety of responses. One uncle said: "Professionals need to be more aware of how overwhelming this is for all the family members. No one ever contacted us." In reassuring contrast, one aunt said: "Finally, I hit upon one psychiatrist who, in my desperation and weeping, said: 'Is there anything that I can do for you?' and I said 'Yes,' and so I was in therapy with her for a year and a half. It was the best thing that ever happened to me." (We do not know if the problems she went into therapy for are related to her niece with SMI, but we include this account as an instance of sensitivity and accessibility on the part of a professional in the field.)

A few more comments were in defense of professionals, as in: "I'm sure that professionals tell people like me that it is not their fault, but probably we just don't hear it, because we are so sure that if only we had done things right, this wouldn't have happened."

Mention should be made that some families refuse help. One nephew described his family as thinking that any professional advice concerning hospitalization or medicine was "nuts." He said about his uncle that "All he needed was fresh air and good nutrition."

This chapter opened with the inspiration of a second cousin as an example of how important even a distant relative might be. In support of this idea, I end with something else this same cousin said: "We grew up across the country from each other, so I hardly knew him when I was growing up. But there is a fond acknowledgment of each other that seems to grow the more we see each other. I hardly know him, so I don't have a sense of what he really feels and thinks. But he likes to tell me jokes, and, well, I feel responsible because he's family and I love my first cousin, and I love him, and I want to see him, and I'll be there for him when he needs me."

Clinical Implications

As with the section on grandparents, I have only twenty interviews on which to base thoughts about how to be most helpful. Our small sample of extended family members was not random, and most of our interviewees were involved and in contact with their respective SMI relatives. Naturally, SMI's ripple effect was clearly evident among these relatives.

A cousin growing up around the extended family cannot be compared to a nephew from another state who has never even met his mentally ill relative. So I make no attempt at generalized clinical implications beyond the obvious one: having an SMI relative deeply affects some extended family members, and we need to be aware of them, both as potential helpers and as people who may need help, information about SMI, and answers to "What is going on?"

Professionals can check with clients to see if extended relatives (or close friends, too) are playing a significant role in the life of the client/consumer with SMI. Professionals in the health care system who routinely include extended family members enlarge the circle of support for most people with SMI—and for their primary caregivers. The greater the circle of support, the better it is for everyone involved. And the more two-way contact between family members and professionals, the better.

As I write this, it is easy to imagine a clinician protesting: "How can I add still more people and more complexities to my list of things to do?" Prior to our twenty interviews, this would have been my reaction.

Now I offer this suggestion. When doing an initial interview with a client or family, just add a question to the effect of: "Are there any extended family members or close friends who you think would benefit from contact with our agency, or could help us with [the person with SMI]?"

By offering clients the opportunity to include significant relatives or friends, you may be able to help someone such as the graduate student described in this chapter's opening paragraph. In turn, this may improve circumstances for the person with SMI as well as for the immediate family.

Reference

Marsh, D. T. (1992). *Families and mental illness: New directions in professional practice.* New York: Praeger.

VII

GRIEF WITHOUT END

> Everyone can cure a grief but he
> who has it.
> —Shakespeare

Trying to capture the essence of grief in writing is like trying to capture the wind in a box or the ocean in a glass. Webster's dictionary says it is a "deep and poignant distress caused by bereavement." So it is—and more. Aside from this feeling of distress, *grief* also refers to a process that evolves over time.

> When losses emerge in our lives, our first
> impulse is not to let go, but to save, to control,
> to cling. Yet it is precisely by doing so that we
> cut ourselves off from life. Only by losing, by
> grieving, by letting go, will we find new life.
> —Sullender (1989, p. 33)

This chapter talks about what we do know about grief (in general as well as from various studies), common myths or misconceptions, and some ideas about the kind of grief process that may unfold concerning an SMI relative. Chapters 9 and 10 talk about coping.

The Nature of Grief

Grief is closely linked to attachment. Human beings have an innate instinct to attach themselves emotionally to people, things, and places—most especially people. We build our lives and identities around attachments to our families, our friends, our roles, our work, our nationalities, and so on. If and when we lose or move away from one of these, we experience a loss. And we are left with the job of finding new meanings and identities for ourselves. This task is one function of the grieving process.

Traditionally, research on grieving has distinguished *sudden grief* (as with loss due to a car accident, murder, or hurricane) from *anticipatory grief* (as with loss due to slow death by cancer or a dementia).

Most biological and psychological studies of grief have focused on the first year of bereavement. For most people, however, the grieving process continues way beyond a year. Various researchers (e.g., Glick et al., 1974; Parkes & Weiss, 1983) have found that people may experience intense grief for an average of two years, and that forms of chronic grief and sorrow may go on forever. We need more longitudinal studies on grieving.

CREATIVE WRITERS ON GRIEF

Eli, Eli, Lama sabaccthani
The battle was over
and the fighter was dead,
when a man came up to him and said,
"Don't die. I love you so much."
But the corpse went on dying.
—Cesar Vallejo

Poets, songwriters, and novelists have paid enormous attention to grief and provide a fascinating contrast to social science research. Turn on any country western radio station and you can hear lyrical attempts to grasp the magnitude of grief. It is clear that living with grief is of paramount importance to people.

While many songs focus on romantic loss, families of people with SMI have their own focus. The journalist and family member Sam Orr (1989, p. 20) writes:

> We parents transit through every available emotion from rage to spontaneous weeping, resolving usually into . . . "perpetual grief" which resides just under the surface for us and for those of our offspring who have accepted their illness and remember what it was like before.

Barton (1969, p. 243) writes of grief: "It takes us very deep down, back perhaps into early childhood or even infancy. It takes with it a whole past, a kind of deprivation one cannot even believe." Endless examples of struggling with this process are available from creative literature, popular culture, and individuals living with grief. Neugeboren (1994, p. 339) writes of his fifty-year-old brother in a mental hospital:

> Seeing Robert like this was not new for me, [but] each time it happened it took me by surprise, and each time it happened, it seemed unutterably sad and heartbreaking.

He wrote this after thirty-one years of his brother's SMI and more hospitalizations than he could count. Similarly, we hear from an anonymous creative writer and parent:

> The world outside: people talking to me, wars, earthquakes, students to teach, papers to write—when grief strikes, all these things seem illusory. The truth is here, now, in this hospital room with my son screaming in hallucinatory terrors, totally unknown to me.

Social science researchers and creative writers present this same contrast in the literature on death and dying (Wasow, 1984). Researchers look for stages and the best way of coping with dying, leading us to believe that if we just do it right, it might not be so bad. Creative writers are saying that dying is the absolute pits. (A noticeable recent exception is Anatole Broyard's 1992 account of his own dying process, in *Intoxicated by My Illness*. Although his message contradicts what I've just written, this book is so excellent that I must mention it.)

MYTHS ABOUT GRIEF

Although human beings have struggled with loss and grief from the dawn of history, it is only within the last fifty years that social scientists have done any systematic research on grieving. Stearns (1984) wrote: "Grief is profoundly misunderstood in American society." This may be a factor in how our culture handles— or tries to avoid—the many feelings and dimensions of recovering from loss.

Many of our misconceptions show up in common sayings and myths such as the examples that follow.

Myth: Grieving has specific steps and stages, and we can move through it in some orderly fashion.

This is a misapplication of Kübler-Ross's (1969) description of how people eventually accept their losses. By oversimplifying the grieving process, we may find it less daunting, but most people do not move through mourning in a linear, stepwise fashion. Also, Kübler-Ross's interviewees were all volunteers—a very biased sample (as is ours).

Myth: Time heals all.

Not only do we underestimate the length of time and the chronicity of certain kinds of grief, but we also underestimate the complexities of it. For example, sadness about those whom we have loved and with whom we have unfinished business often remains with us forever.

One reason for ongoing grief is that we rarely reach complete emotional acceptance of loss. "Few among the bereaved ever arrive at a time when they are no longer susceptible to a flash of memory of a sudden association that subjects them again to intense pain" (Parkes & Weiss, 1983, p. 157). We continue being vulnerable to pangs of grief, and this is normal as long as it does not interfere with our general daily functioning. To have a few minutes or even an hour disrupted does not mean that grief has impaired our daily functioning.

Myth: "You should be over this by now."

We strive to get over grief, but that may be impossible. In some situations, such as grieving for a relative lost to mental illness, we might be more realistic in trying to accept the inevitability of our grief. After all, how can we resolve something that neither remains the same nor goes away?

Myth: "It's not healthy for you to keep going over and over this. You need to keep busy."

Repeatedly reviewing events connected to loss is often necessary for emotional acceptance. This process can be painful for friends and relatives, as well as the more immediately bereaved. Because it is hard to feel comfortable around a grieving person, others may urge us to get on with our lives way too soon. This leaves us alone in our grieving. As Parkes and Weiss observe (1983, p. 159):

> It takes sensitivity and, perhaps, experience to distinguish between the normal process of recovery in which there is a slow but steady movement in review, and chronic grief, in which obsessive review is unbudging. And it takes great tolerance for another's pain to be accepting of either.

In short, our society's myths exert lots of pressure to amputate or hide our ongoing grief. Such myths and misconceptions usually spring up when people feel uncomfortable and face gaps in their knowledge. The more we learn about the grieving process, the better equipped we will be to recognize and accept our own—and each other's—experiences, needs, and feelings.

SMI and Grief

Another gap in knowledge has to do specifically with SMI and grieving. To date, just one preliminary study exists on unresolved grief in families of people with SMI (Miller et al., 1990). This team found a "surprisingly low level of initial grief but higher levels of present grief" (p. 1321). Grief in these families actually increased over time. Many people may experience an undulating pattern of grief, in which feelings get stronger or more painful over time, then lessen a bit, and then continue intensifying and waning over the decades.

Grieving about a relative with mental illness is a special subcategory. First, it involves a family member. Second, it involves chronic loss. Third, it involves the brain. And it is profoundly misunderstood in this culture.

FAMILY MEMBERS

A loss within the family creates an intensity and longevity of grieving unlike any other loss. For better or worse, it is usually within the family that we experience our closest bonds and greatest love (as well as our highest murder rates). The closer the bond, the more profound the grief we feel over any misfortune or loss. Then, because many family members are grieving at the same time and are absorbed by their own sorrows, they often have no strength left over for each other (MacGregor, 1994).

Furthermore, as MacGregor wrote with regard to an SMI child, "grief changes people, and so in the midst of their depression and despair, both parents face adjusting to being with a changed spouse" (p. 162). If this phenomenon takes place between spouses, surely it also occurs among other relatives, and emotional effects thus ripple throughout the family. Everyone ends up facing "a complex reorganization of lifestyle, self-perception, role, economic security, and belief systems, and all of this process involves loss" (p. 163).

Modifying our self-perception can be especially painful, as MacGregor (p. 163) exemplified in this passage:

> I grieved because in a time of adversity I
> proved to be less noble and more vulnerable
> and needy than I had thought myself to be. I
> grieved because I could not be a comforter . . .
> to others. I grieved simply because sorrow
> had entered my life.

Whichever way it goes, or however it arises, grief within the family is uniquely powerful.

CHRONICITY

SMI grief is also in a special category because it wells up in response to an ongoing illness. Chronic conditions entail chronic grief, rather than sudden or anticipatory grief. To think in terms of anticipating death or loss while the person with SMI still lives is to run the risk of feeling guilty about abandoning him or her. On the other hand, something surely had been lost. It is a complex situation for families to experience and sort out.

With ongoing conditions such as SMI, developmental disabilities, and permanent physical disabilities, friends and family may not find any closure on their grieving process. Since afflicted members do not die or disappear when they develop SMI, we face our loss every time we face our child, our parent, our spouse, our sibling, or our other SMI relative. Our sorrow is strong and continuing.

MacGregor (1994) described cyclical patterns in the grief experienced over mental illness in a loved one. These cycles of grief can surface at any time, especially during a crisis. Even many years down the road, our grief can be as intense or even more intense than at diagnosis. It is almost as if an allergic response has set in. Once someone's body has been traumatized by an allergic reaction to a bee sting, for instance, the next sting can get the whole body into an uproar. Likewise, we can have "allergic" emotional reactions. A new crisis can send an individual or a family into renewed feelings of intense grief. "Oh lord, here we go again!"

Another major problem for relatives grieving for their SMI loved ones is that our society does not recognize this grief. As MacGregor wrote (1994, p. 164):

> [People like us] have joined an underclass of
> grievers disenfranchised by society from the
> normal grieving process, because their loss is
> not openly acknowledged, publicly mourned,
> or socially supported.

He also pointed out that mental health professionals seldom address grief responses of families to a relative with SMI. Or if they do, they frequently misperceive the ever-renewing grief as evidence of pathology. Parents in particular are well aware of and fearful of being pathologized, so they may inhibit any expression of their grief. This makes matters even worse for them, "because it can interfere significantly with a parent's ability to move forward emotionally and deal effectively with the uncertainty that lies ahead" (p. 161).

Parkes and Weiss (1983) suggested that continuing grief may serve as a means of restitution. That is, because we cannot help or cure a loved one, we may try to make it up by grieving forever. We mourn not only for the person who was, but also for the person who would have been and now never will be. We do not get over such grief; we get used to it.

THE BRAIN

Finally, families face a special kind of grief because SMI affects the brain. The mind is what makes us human, what distinguishes us from all other mammals. Change the brain, and you change the human capacity in many respects. These illnesses thus create agony not only for the stricken but for their entire family. We lose our original relationships with SMI relatives, as well as our dreams and beliefs about their futures.

Mourning our losses is complicated by the fact that communicating with the SMI relative becomes more difficult than usual. Much confusion ensues when we interact with someone who looks the same but in many ways is not. Nor does it help that neither the SMI nor the grief is recognized by society. As one parent poignantly put it, "I grieved because my son seemed to have no place in a world too ignorant and weak to cure him and perhaps too hostile to care" (MacGregor, 1991, p. 163). All in all, families are left feeling inadequate, misunderstood, and isolated.

Unresolved SMI Grief

As coping with SMI involves a special category of grief, not much of the literature offers useful models of this process. For instance, in writing about death and grief, Viorst (1986) said: "So perhaps the only choice we have is to choose what to do with our dead: To die when they die. To live crippled. Or to forge, out of pain and memory, new adaptations" (p. 264).

Can we apply this standard bereavement model to grief over SMI? Probably not, for several reasons. First, such a model is predicted on an actual death, which is tangible and receives social acceptance. Second, it fails to acknowledge the family members' lifetime commitment to and efforts concerning their ill relative. Third, we are dealing with both actual and symbolic loss, and families have no time-bound stages of grief to move through. The end result for them is often unresolved grief.

The risks of unresolved grief are many. If we do not find ways to cope with loss, we run the risk of getting locked into our sorrow, or even trapped by it. This is called *unresolved* or *abnormal grief*. "Clinically, abnormal grief has all the characteristics of idolatry. If we cannot successfully grieve the loss of something or someone, we may make it into an idol" (Sullender, 1989, p. 33).

That is, we long for the person and desperately want back the qualities that have evaporated. We believe that this alone can restore our happiness—if only he or she would return to a former way of being. We simply cannot let go. The lost person becomes revered and starts to control our lives and energies. In the process of idolizing and hanging on to the past, we not only get stuck in our grief but also tend to deaden our own lives. We stop living.

By contrast, as Feldman and Kornfield wrote in *Stories of the Spirit, Stories of the Heart* (1991, p. 331): "It is when we are no longer afraid of loss that we begin to open in a wholehearted way to the world around us." Some of us can also relate to this in terms of a lost love affair, which we eventually get over as the object of our love goes away.

A loved one with SMI does not go away, however, so we have a harder time getting over the loss. Families may have a delayed grief reaction, reflecting the difficulty of mourning in situations other than death. Regarding parents of handicapped children and mothers who give up their babies for adoption (Simos, 1979), and family members of patients with Alzheimer's Disease (Wasow, 1985), studies have suggested that the resolution of grief for such relatives differs from those of people who mourn a death. Relatives may continue to hope for a cure or much more improvement than is likely to occur, thus prolonging the onset of grief. This might reflect the progressive nature of these SMI patients' illnesses. As time and the illnesses go on, the patient and family suffer more and more losses.

> Finally, families of severely mentally ill persons
> may not fully appreciate their loss until years
> later, when they have had time to truly under-

stand the deleterious effects of the illness on
their children and siblings.
　　　　　—Miller et al. (1990), p. 1324

　　Difficulties in recovering from loss are more frequent in
conflict-ridden relationships, which are almost inevitable when
dealing with people who have SMI. In writing about bereavement,
Parkes and Weiss (1983) referred to the "conflicted grief syndrome"
as including generalized anxiety, self-doubt, and distress.

　　As Marsh (1992, p. 92) elaborated: "Unresolved grief is
usually accompanied by a variety of symptoms, including depression, hostility, guilt and self-reproach, somatic problems, and an
absence of emotional and social re-entry." This has a high cost,
obviously. Yet we can hardly wonder that unresolved SMI grief
prevails under current circumstances: lack of knowledge or information about severe mental illness, among professionals, friends
and families of the SMI, and the public at large; lack of understanding or compassion for the chronic mourning that ensues; and
outright prejudice, hostility, and even ostracism aimed at the
severely mentally ill and their families.

　　Living with grief can be intensely difficult. Dealing with
the complexities of SMI adds a host of negative emotions to the
process. There are so many unknowns concerning SMI, and the
manifestations of the illnesses keep changing, making adjustment
and adaptation all the more difficult. This is not to say that family
members cannot rise above their grief, but rather to point out that it
is a particularly difficult grief. We must be merciful on ourselves.

Toward a Model for SMI Grieving

　　To move out of our current circumstances, the first thing
we need is to study and understand more about SMI grief and how it
unfolds over time. I have questioned the traditional concept of
orderly stages, pointing out the complexities and uniqueness of
grief over losing a loved one to mental illness. Now I will present

how we sensed our interviewees coped with the intensity of grieving over time, given the ups and downs of the illness, the circumstances of their lives, and the extent of our abilities (or lack thereof) to build meaningful lives out of chaos.

Early and later grief reactions usually differ. In initial reactions to trauma and grief, the mind has a great deal of work to do to come to terms with the new reality. Two very different things tend to happen. One extreme is to avoid the facts; the other, to preoccupy ourselves with them, often reexperiencing traumatic events. The mind is working hard to assimilate what has happened and to integrate it with previous experience.

During (and after) the beginning stages of the SMI, many family members painfully question decisions they make under the stress. Starting from a position of ignorance about the illness, they naturally develop dependency on professional judgment. That professional judgment, benign at best, is often downright harmful. Many professionals do not recognize SMI in its earliest stages. Neither does anyone else, but professionals need to be more humble in their pronouncements. This is a terribly confusing time for all concerned.

It is doubly hard for families to feel they did the best they could when harmful things have been done to their loved ones, as well as to themselves. As one parent put it: "Typically, we try a number of inappropriate therapists and counseling until there is a full-blown psychotic episode that initiates the Kafka-trek through the public system" (Orr, 1989, p. 20).

These early years are fraught with desperate searching for answers, "cures," resources within the community, hopes, false hopes, arguments within the family about how to best handle things, denial, acceptance, more denial, and so on. The family system reels under the impact of subjective and objective burdens. Lowered life satisfaction follows for all concerned. Overprotectiveness, emotional disengagement, scapegoating, diminished self-esteem, societal stigma, and dissolution of the family can and often do occur.

An experience of dual loss is taking place: of the person who was, and of the person who will never be. Additionally, many family members share an empathic grief with the ill relative, whom they sense is also mourning and grieving for his or her own lost hopes and dreams.

People vary in their ability to tolerate emotional arousal and distressing emotions, both on a psychological and physiological level. The most frequently cited reactions to grief are:

Sleep disturbance
Disrupted appetite
Muscle tension
Anxiety
Depression
Crying
Anger
Problems with concentration and judgment
Mental preoccupation with the loss
Guilt

Social withdrawal and giving up previously enjoyable activities are also frequent reactions to grief.

People vary enormously because they differ in their constitutional makeup and because of the many, many circumstantial variations in all our lives. The personality and degree of illness of the SMI relative, the ages of all family members, the economic situation, community resources, religious beliefs, support networks, and other factors in daily life all affect how one survives or sinks under the grieving process.

For some family members, the frantic searching lessens as they learn more about the illness. Less chaos and desperation may prevail over time. But this may also deepen the grief. That is, as long as we are frantically searching, our energy is distracted away from grief. For some, giving up on hope for a cure is a turning point. It is the beginning of acceptance. I repeat, "for some."

Some people manage to recover rather well from the protracted grieving process, and some are even strengthened by it. For a large variety of reasons, however, many others suffer lasting damage to body, mind, and soul. As many variables affect the outcome as there are people, but friends and family play a crucial role in our adaptation to loss and grief. The substantial research on psychological recovery consistently shows the importance of social supports. Positive support helps us feel cared for and validated; it offers an avenue for expressing our feelings.

Our culture's responses to mental illnesses are stigmatizing and hostile. If, in addition, some of our friends and family also do not understand, this can create a secondary injury to us. This is why groups such as the Alliance for the Mentally Ill are so important to our well-being; they are places we can count on for validation.

Time usually lessens and numbs pain, but grief does not automatically go away if we ignore it. Time heals, but it does not remove scars. The process is long and uneven and, while the general tendency may be upward, the process usually involves periodic bouts of depression, yearning, loneliness, guilt, anxiety, sadness, frustration, desperation, and anger. Upsets are often interspersed with increasngly longer periods of relief and well-being.

Sometimes it is best to be in touch with our feelings. At other times, it may be more helpful to modulate overwhelming feelings by partial denial, "numbing out," and distancing ourselves. No formula tells us when to use what—other than the suggestion that there is nothing to be gained by feeling overwhelmed. As Garrison Keillor (1987) would say: "Some days you just have to stare reality in the face—and deny it."

Not all reactions are unremittingly sad. I am reminded of a deeply touching few moments during a workshop on grieving, years ago in Alaska. The participants were a group of twenty upbeat, friendly, older frontier-type Alaskans. We had been having a lovely day together, with lots of good laughs. These people were all older parents of adult children who were developmentally disabled. Many of them had been coping for forty years or longer. At one point in the conversation, a participant said: "Sometimes I think I'm nuts. I flip through the TV channels every day looking for a soap opera I can cry over for a few minutes. Of course, I'm really just using this as an excuse to cry over Emily. Am I nuts or what?" (Emily was forty years old and had been developmentally disabled since birth. Her parents were in their mid-seventies.)

"I don't know," I said, "but I'm curious about how many of you have had similar experiences with crying almost every day, even if only for a moment of two?" All the participants raised their hands in agreement. We all looked around the room and smiled at each other with amusement, camaraderie, and relief.

This intrigued me so much that, over and over again through the years at workshops, I have asked that question of parents of chronically disabled children. While I cannot give you statistics on the subject, the responses are always the same. Hundreds of parents have answered affirmatively.

In short, the majority of parents may cry on an almost daily basis about their ill child. This does not mean throwing ourselves down on the bed and weeping for hours, or even with much intensity. It may be only a fleeting moment of tears. Our pain brims near the surface and is ever present.

This does not preclude living lives of satisfaction and joy. We can experience chronic sorrow and simultaneously lead happy, fulfilling lives. It is not an either/or situation. Human beings are amazingly flexible sometimes, and we can do all sorts of things at once. The abilities of many people to emerge from grim, unresolvable situations and salvage good lives for themselves are inspiring.

Summary

In a society that is more inclined to help us hide our pain than live through it, we need to make a conscious effort to mourn. Before we try to understand how to cope with our pain (as discussed in chapter 9), we need to come to terms with our SMI grief and acknowledge our profound, constant experience of loss. Otherwise, the pain may boomerang and catch us somewhere else.

We will have times of maudlin tears and moments of pure agony. Sometimes grief becomes so intense it feels like fear, like suspense, like waiting for something dreadful to happen. Sometimes it is very quiet. Mostly, life does not seem worth the effort while we are in the grip of grief. We do not want to start anything, cannot settle down; we yawn and fidget. Maybe we eat or drink or smoke too much. I am not saying we should wallow in this; we need to get out from under the pain, at times. But at other times, we may live through it, not be afraid, and know that it will pass.

Grief is a most uncomfortable emotion. There are no magic ways of preventing, resolving, or curing it. Nor does any rule or law say we cannot have a good life in spite of it. All of us—clinicians, family members, educators, and people living with mental illnesses—can try to keep the faith.

References

Broyard, A. (1992). *Intoxicated by my illness*. New York: Clarkson Potter.

Feldman, C., & Kornfield, J. (Eds.) (1991). *Stories of the spirit, stories of the heart: Stories of the spiritual path from around the world*. New York: Harper Collins.

Glick, I. O., Weiss, R. S., & Parkes, C. M. (1974). *The first year of bereavement*. New York: Wiley.

Keillor, G. (1987). Prairie home companion. Radio show. St. Paul, MN.

Ku¨ bler-Ross, E. (1969). *On death and dying*. New York: Macmillan.

MacGregor, P. (1994, Mar.). Grief: The unrecognized parental response to mental illness in a child. *Social Work, 39*(2), 160–166.

Marsh, D. (1992). *Families and mental illness.* New York: Praeger.

Miller, F., Dworkin, J., Ward, M., & Barone, D. (1990). A preliminary study of unresolved grief in families of SMI patients. *Hospital and Community Psychology, 41*(12), 1321–25.

Neugeboren, J. (1994, Sum.). Meanwhile, back on the ward. *The American Scholar,* 337–348.

Nouwen, J. M. (1980, Jan.). *In memoriam.* Notre Dame, IN: Ave Maria Press.

Orr, S. (1989, Nov.). Homelessness: A family perspective. *The California Psychologist,* n.p.

Parkes, C. M., & Weiss, R. S. (1983). *Recovery from bereavement.* New York: Basic Books.

Potok, A. (1980). *Ordinary daylight: Portrait of an artist going blind.* New York: Holt, Rinehart & Winston.

Sarton, M. (1989). *The education of Harriet Hatfield.* New York: Norton.

Shakespeare, W. *Much ado about nothing,* act III, sc. 2: 28.

Simos, B. G. (1984). *A time to grieve.* New York: Family Service Association of America (44 East 23rd Street, NY 10010).

Stearns, A. K. (1984) *Living through personal crises.* Chicago: Thomas Moore Press.

Sullender, R. (1989). *Losses in later life.* Mahwah, NJ: Integration Books/Paulist Press.

Viorst, J. (1986). *Necessary losses.* New York: Ballantine Books.

Wasow, M. (1985). Chronic schizophrenia and Alzheimer's disease: The losses for parents, spouses, and children compared. *Journal of Chronic Diseases, 38*(8): 711–716.

Wasow, M. (1984). Get out of my potato patch: A biased view of death and dying. *Health and Social Work, 9*(4): 261–267.

VIII

SAYING IT OUT LOUD JUST ONCE

> I not only have my secrets, I am
> my secrets. And you are your
> secrets. Our secrets are human
> secrets, and our trusting each
> other enough to share them with
> each other has much to do with
> the secret of what it is to be
> human.
> —Beucher (1991, p. 33)

Several years ago at an AMI state conference, I gave a talk on "Coping." I introduced the topic by saying: "You are giving me a good honorarium, so I must be an expert. Indeed, I do know the coping literature, and I had been very good at coping during the three years my son with SMI lived in a group home two thousand miles away from me. But two weeks ago he returned to my home, and now I'm falling apart at the seams: weeping, not sleeping well, nervous, eating too much, irritable, scared about the future." The audience laughed enthusiastically and applauded, the first time I was ever applauded before starting a talk! Their response conveyed a strong message.

Over the years, I have participated in endless discussions with family members, hearing and speaking some of the bleakest words imaginable. Many of us do not feel safe uttering strong, negative, culturally frowned-upon feelings in front of anyone other than fellow family members. Who knows how such utterances would be interpreted? We express them out loud in the safety of others who have been there. We are emerging from the family-bashing era, and it seems just yesterday that parents were accused of scapegoating their children with SMI. So how could we publicly say, "Sometimes I feel that he'd be better off dead"?

Dark thoughts and wishes surely occur at times for all people. The words in this chapter will not surprise many readers, but it is interesting to contemplate why very little research examines this aspect of coping with SMI. Most academic disciplines either ignore the topic of dark thoughts or treat them in accordance with the rationalist tradition, as with a psychoanalytic interpretation. A more recent view comes from neuroscience, which contributes to the negative valuation of these thoughts by reducing them to no more than biochemical excitations.

Consequently, for the most part, dark thoughts remain the province of poets, novelists, and filmmakers. Strong emotions, passions, and bleak thoughts fascinate us. Such books, films, and television programs attract wide audiences.

> Perhaps the enormous appeal of fiction, film, and psychotherapy in our time is that they are almost the only permissible cultural channels of unrestrained subjectivity and feelings. They accept, endorse, and validate the immense importance of that which science dismisses with a condescending wave of a hand. They emphasize the importance of the inner experience, of subjectivity.
> —Person (1989, p. 20)

Although science and scientific methods have enormous prestige in our age, they also have a propensity to value only those things they can explain. Rich inner experiences do not always lend themselves to controlled studies. As the psychoanalyst Person

(1989) points out: "But that dismissal of what does not seem amenable to testing, quantification, verification, and replication, of what is judged to be sentimental or biased on feeling, is itself often pseudoscientific and irrational" (p. 19). Insisting on the scientific method denies the limits of reason and reason's easy distortion by unconscious forces. Even so, the scientific point of view remains very powerful, and it tends to ignore the immense importance of passions and feelings in our lives. Too often we "blink away the actualities of our condition, the feelings, drives, dreams, and desires that express, with painful accuracy, the depths at which we really live" (Person, p. 19).

We try to deny these dark thoughts, or at least keep them at bay. We may not know what to do with them, or we may want to wallow in misery. But getting ourselves to think and reinterpret negative thoughts in a kinder and less critical frame of reference is often helpful. Positive thinking is a good coping mechanism and a fine way of living when we can do it; but the first step in this direction, ironically, can be to allow ourselves to experience and acknowledge the depth of our despair. Simply accepting our hard feelings as an understandable reaction to a miserable situation often removes the power of their pain. Bleak thoughts exist, they are allowed, they will pass, and they do not kill. There is a big difference between thoughts and actions. Sometimes our thoughts feel so hurtful that, as children often do, we react to our thoughts and feelings by thinking we are guilty of some crime. To repeat: bad thoughts are not evil.

I have spent twenty years devoted to my son who has an SMI, to the NAMI movement, to training students in this area, and to fighting stigma in our country. Speaking of saying awful things out loud: his agony has made my career!

Many years ago, I was sitting with a dear friend whose son also had schizophrenia. We admitted to each other that we sometimes wished our sons were dead, so that we could see an end to the suffering for all concerned. A few years later, her son did die; and when we next met, I asked: "Do you remember our conversation of a few years ago?"

"Of course I do," she replied.

"And now?" I asked.

Her eyes filled with tears: "Oh, I'd do anything to have him back." That scene comes to mind very often. I wonder how I would really feel if my son died.

Over the years, I have spoken with family members around the country, especially at NAMI meetings. We have all spoken desperate words, which remain seared in my memory. A sixty-year-old father once said of his SMI child's suicide of ten years past: "The pain gets worse with time, not better." I have also heard just the opposite. People are different. The most common words spoken after a death seem to be "If only." If only we had done this, or that, or if there had been better community care, or if the hospital had kept her, or if . . ..

"Do not ever give up hope," one parent said to another, who replied: "The sum total of the ignorance and impotence of mental health and legal systems have finally liberated me from all hope."

A mother from London said: "I wish a lorry would run the poor thing down and not let him suffer any more."

In response, her friend said: "I'm so desperate that I'd take off to Australia with the little ones, without leaving an address."

A father added: "Occasionally you get a flash of the person that was, and that is even worse than when he is totally out of it."

From an adult sibling: "I wish for a policy of euthanasia for persons . . . with schizophrenia."

As for risky experimental treatments: "I don't care how risky it is. I'd rather she were dead, really" (Schulz et al., 1982, p. 507).

"I'm so ashamed of how she looks and acts and smells. I'm embarrassed to be seen with her. Then I hate myself for being ashamed," said a forty-five-year-old parent.

"I pretended that she wasn't my sister. Like a Judas, I denied her."

"I cannot believe that a God of love and mercy willed my father's suicide; it was my father himself who willed it as the only way out available to him from a life that he had come to find unbearable."

Sometimes, tragically, people do translate thoughts of desperation into action. A 1989 headline in the *Ledger* newspaper of Columbia, South Carolina read: "Murder: North Carolina family's final solution for mentally ill son." The article said that for sixteen years the family had tried to get him help. They got him into hospitals, but once in the hospital he was badly raped, so they tried to get him out. The entire family was torn apart. They had no resources in the community or within their own family. Their son was the fourth of ten children in this rural, poor black family. "He loved to read and brought home report cards full of A's and B's." In the last of the many horrors, he was raped again in the hospital and so the mother got him out. He threatened the family with violence, and everyone was exhausted. His mother and sister planned his death, reportedly. The sister who shot him was weeping and her mother was saying, "He's better off now. There's nothing else we could have done." The daughter was put away in prison for life.

This is a tragedy for all concerned, and it is beyond the realm of dark thoughts. Shooting is certainly not the solution for anything. So why include this story in a sad litany of quotations? To remind us all that families are up against situations that often have no solutions, are desperate beyond belief, and often get no help whatsoever from the community.

Horrible things can and sometimes do happen under such circumstances. We must never act out our dark thoughts. But we can be more merciful to ourselves by accepting the legitimacy of our feelings.

This material is hard to write. To family members, I want to say: you are not alone. *There is absolutely nothing to be gained from "saying it out loud" to people who have SMIs.* But we can tell each other. To educators, my message is: tell students the stories of family members and encourage them to read literature written by relatives of the SMI. There is no substitute for this. To the frontline clinicians, many of whom have their own dark thoughts and need to be heard: be aware of the depth of despair many families feel. (You probably already are, but just in case . . ..)

As for people with SMI, the sad truth is that their burden of sadness and desperation is even greater. Also, many SMI people are well aware of their family's pain, and try to protect them from it. In the book *Telling Secrets* (1991, p. 33), Beucher writes:

> The sad things that happened long ago will always remain part of who we are just as the glad and gracious things will too, but instead of being a burden of guilt, recrimination, and regret that make us constantly stumble as we go, even the saddest things can become, once we have made peace with them, a source of wisdom and strength for the journey that still lies ahead.

Secrets and bleak thoughts are important because they tell us what we really feel and yearn for: to be known in our full humanness. Paradoxically, they are often what we also fear more than anything else. But it is important to be honest, for to do otherwise is to lose track of who we really are.

> My story is important not because it is mine, God knows, but because if I tell it anything like right, the chances are you will recognize that in many ways it is also yours. Maybe nothing is more important than that we keep track, you and I, of these stories . . . to lose track of our stories is to be profoundly impoverished.
> —Beucher (1991, p. 30)

References

Beucher, F. (1991). *Telling secrets*. New York: Harper Books.
The Ledger (1989, Feb. 27). Columbia, SC.
Person, E. (1989). *Dreams of love and fateful encounters: The power of romantic passion*. New York: Penguin.
Schulz, P. M., Schulz, S. C., Dibble, E., Targum, S. D., van Kammen, D. P., & Gerson, E. S. (1982). Patient and family attitudes about schizophrenia: Implications for genetic counseling. *Schizophrenia Bulletin, 9*(3) 504–513.

IX

COPING AND CONTROL

It is a particularly North American notion that people should be able to manage negative feelings and be happy most of the time. Most cultures in this world accept that life is often a struggle; our expectation that it should be otherwise probably compounds our troubles. For example, consider what we know about the Christmas holidays in the United States. One cultural belief is that we should all be having a Norman Rockwell holiday season full of joy and love. Since this does not usually happen for many, the discrepancy is enormous. The resulting pain in the five weeks between Thanksgiving and New Year's makes for high rates of suicide, depression, and general violence.

Along with the idea that life should be good if we just do things right—as in "children will turn out fine if we raise them right"—another belief is that we have control over our destiny. It is hard for us to accept that bad things happen to good people. In his excellent book *The Coping Capacity* (1984), the psychoanalyst Avery Weisman emphasized the foolishness of leading people to believe that if they could just "get it all together," their lives would be smooth and happy. Life is full of unpredictable events entirely outside our control: everything from earthquakes and hurricanes and getting hit by drunk drivers to schizophrenia and holes in the ozone. We do *not* have control over much that happens in our lives; and therefore, says Weisman, our aim should be to increase our coping capacity, rather than futilely attempting to control things over which we have no control. This notion is quite applicable to coping with the stresses of mental illness in the family.

Having things outside our control forces us to face the existential crises of unpredictability and meaninglessness. Most of us have trouble dealing with the arbitrariness of bad luck. We live in a fix-it society, but strong feelings cannot be fixed in the way a broken windowpane is fixed. After experiencing a shattering loss that cannot be fixed—such as the death of a loved one, a mental illness, or the Chernobyl nuclear disaster—we learn just how vulnerable we are, and how capable of profound suffering. After that, the world never feels entirely safe again. Understanding and accepting our lack of control allows us to move on to increase our coping capacity.

This chapter looks at some of the ways we deal with shattered beliefs. It also looks at the dominant and destructive role of guilt, and the role of anger. Finally, since we have little control over life's events, I offer suggestions for increasing our coping capacities.

Dealing with Shattered Beliefs

How do people come to grips with severe trauma or bereavement? Most of us believe in a just world, in which we get what we deserve. We are therefore deeply threatened by random negative events. One way we try to hold on to our basic assumptions is to blame ourselves: "If we had just raised our children right, this would not have happened." Such an attitude can be seen as neurotic and dysfunctional; or we can view it as a healthy attempt to hang on to our beliefs about the world as a safe and predictable place; we just did not do the right things.

In 1992 Bulman did a study of paralyzed survivors of accidents and made a surprising finding: self-blame was associated with high levels of coping. Even though these people had been involved in freak accidents and were not at fault, those who reacted by blaming themselves showed better coping patterns. Bulman felt that self-blame reflected the struggle of survivors to make sense of their victimization and to understand "Why me?" It also minimized the threat of randomness in their world. Car accidents and losing a loved one to severe mental illness are not the same, but it is interesting to consider the possibility that, in both cases, self-blame can be a way of maintaining equilibrium in the face of shattered beliefs about our world.

People use a variety of strategies to cope with and rebuild shattered beliefs; to somehow integrate the old ("The world is safe") and the new ("Tragedy can strike at random"). One time-honored method is to make appraisals based on comparisons with others, particularly other victims. If misery loves company, it loves miserable company even more. Another strategy is to examine and interpret our role in the tragedy. Here most of us run the gamut from self-blame ("If only I had . . .") to the realization that severe mental illnesses are brain disabilities that can and do strike anyone, and that therefore we play no role in their development.

Many of us cope by reevaluating our experience in terms of benefits and purpose. Surely the mental illness offers no benefit to the sufferer, but many family members say things such as: "This has made me more tolerant [stronger/kinder/wiser]." For some of us, it has formed our career choice or volunteer activities. As Bulman wrote (1992, p. 118): "Survivors' reappraisals locate and create evidence of benevolence, meaning, and self-worth in the events that first challenged and shattered their illusions."

If we can manage to take shattering events and turn them around to work *for* us, instead of against us, we are well on the road to recovery. Many touching examples exist of our human ability to do this. To name just a few: the civil rights movements, the consumers movement among people with mental illnesses, advocates for battered women, and of course our own National Alliance for the Mentally Ill.

Guilt and Anger

One of the big problems with mental illness is the long time it takes to make a correct diagnosis. In its beginning stages, mental illness can be hard to distinguish from a difficult adolescence, for instance; and dreadful things may go on between family members during those years between onset and diagnosis. It is not anyone's fault, but we end up feeling very sad about all that happened before we knew what we were dealing with.

Guilt is present in any grief. For parents dealing with a child's mental illness, it is heightened by their sense of responsibility for the child's well-being. "The inability to protect their son or daughter results in a serious loss of self-esteem" (MacGregor, 1994). Compounding this throughout our culture is the ignorance that blames people for mental illness. So families face the double whammy of ignorance and the difficulties in getting a correct diagnosis, which create the ideal fermenting grounds for unremitting guilt. "Guilt," as Erma Bombeck said, "is the gift that keeps on giving!"

Guilt is a miserable, destructive, and unproductive emotion. To ameliorate it, we can ask ourselves a few key questions:

- Did I do the best I knew how, under my particular set of circumstances?
- Could I have known that he/she was developing a mental illness?
- Was I being hurtful on purpose, or just trying to keep my loved one on course?

Give some serious thought to your answers.

Some of our guilt *may* be realistic. In our pain, anger, fear, and frustration, we may have done some very hurtful things. We are only human, and to be human is to err. We are not perfect, so we need to forgive and make peace with ourselves. This is not always easy and does take time, but it is very important to do.

Unrealistic guilt around thoughts of preventability and feelings of powerlessness usually causes anger, and our safest target for such anger is ourselves. We often express it as guilt or depression. Sometimes we turn the anger against a spouse, another child, or the mentally ill relative; sometimes, against the mental health system (often with good reason). Those who are really talented can turn it in all directions at once, but this is not to be recommended.

To move beyond feelings of guilt, it helps to get unstuck from "If only I had . . .." Wishing to alter the past is a dead-end street. When we wander into it, we need to stop and turn around. We also need to understand and accept that it is outside the realm of anybody's power to determine which persons develop mental illnesses and which do not. Given our human limitations, it is not possible to have been everywhere and done everything for our SMI relative. We did the best we knew how.

Another word about anger. It is normal and inevitable, but we are taught from earliest childhood that it is a bad feeling and that we will be punished if we express it directly (as in, "Go to your room and don't come out until . . ."). After an entire childhood of this, most of us reach adulthood with few skills for handling anger—our own or anyone else's. In fact, we often do not even recognize anger when we feel it; it just goes underground and resurfaces as depression, confusion, guilt, anxiety, or something else.

By the same token, feeling angry is often a sign that we are facing our situation, pluses as well as minuses, rather than denying parts of it. For coping with loss, anger is usually more appropriate than depression or guilt. Generally speaking, guilt just wears us down and accomplishes nothing. Anger, put to constructive use, can be an effective tool for advocacy.

So how can we use our anger? To begin, we can try to recognize it for what it is: a feeling. We do not need to bury it or get rid of it. Our thoughts and feelings are free, and we do not need to blame or impose penalties on ourselves for having them.

Then we can find ways of expressing ourselves so that our anger does not boomerang back at us. Easier said than done. We often are punished if we express it angrily, alas. Socially acceptable means of dealing with anger include talking with an understanding friend or a professional. This helps validate what we are feeling, and then maybe we can feel less crazy or bad. Expressing our anger clearly, directly, and in calm tones may also help.

Coping

Coping strategies evolve over years. What works for one person at one time may not work at another. Denying, searching, harboring false hopes, giving up hope, raging, distancing—each has its time and place. It is important to recognize when and where in the process we are (in the first six months, or twenty-five years down the road?). This makes a big difference in what we are dealing with and how many ways of coping we have found, tried, or invented so far.

Strategies are not all that change. Over time, the symptoms of the person with SMI keep changing, the mental health system changes, and so do we and our loved ones. What worked last year may not work today, and what works today may not work next year. This is another reason that coping is a process and an individually crafted repertoire rather than one set of skills.

Dealing with SMI in our loved ones involves constant coping, and we can subdivide this immense process in all sorts of ways, including:

- When we cope: before something occurs (*anticipatory coping*), or afterward (*reactive coping*)
- With what we cope: e.g., with events or symptoms, with external circumstances, or with feelings such as grief
- With whom we cope: with ourselves, friends, professionals, etc.

Other categories abound, but the point here is that we can sort out and understand rather than feel overwhelmed by the ongoing process of encountering and handling SMI's stressful ripples. The ensuing sections look at only a few of the categories of coping, with the hope that this will stimulate your own thinking about being a consumer, family member, or clinician who deals with SMI.

ANTICIPATORY COPING AND REACTIVE COPING

In *anticipating* what could go wrong, we have time to think things through and plan our strategies. In *reactive* coping, we have to be fast on our feet, and at the same time try not to panic or overreact. These two kinds of coping surely demand different skills from us. It is one thing to sit quietly in a room with several good people, planning for a smooth transition into a group home. It is quite another thing to keep our wits about us when a loved one is in the midst of a volatile psychotic break, the police are banging on the front door, and little brother is running out the back.

Obviously, I have no magic formula to suggest for reactive coping, other than the obvious. Have emergency telephone numbers handy, such as the physician in charge, the case manager (if there is one), the police, crisis intervention, and a close friend or relative. Beforehand, give some thought to the sorts of things that help you cope in a crisis. Pay attention also to what helps you recover after a crisis. Not to wish frequent crises on anybody, but with practice we often do get better at coping.

COPING WITH CIRCUMSTANCES

When we have enough time to anticipate problems, we can try a variety of behaviors for coping with symptoms and external circumstances, including modifying our situation and managing our situation.

Modifying our situation means changing outer circumstances, such as a schedule or other living arrangement. *Managing our situation* means changing the way we relate to our circumstances, ourselves, and the people around us. It might include giving ourselves breaks, finding more support (within or beyond our existing resources), or letting go of some of the beliefs that have trapped us into automatic reactions and feeling badly about ourselves.

Studying parents with adult SMI children, Greenley et al. (1989) found five types of coping:

1. Motivational strategies—encouraging their children
2. Positive sanctioning—consistently acknowledging and appreciating each desirable behavior
3. Negative sanctioning—consistently acknowledging and being assertive in response to undesirable behavior

4. Social prevention—avoiding social situations that usually produce tension and stress
5. Physical prevention—avoiding being in a closed space with a person who is highly agitated and/or having hallucinations

The more of these coping strategies we combine, the better. And the more we let each other know about what works in our respective situations, the more choices we have for shaping our daily world.

COPING WITH OURSELVES

Coping with ourselves includes recognizing (or discovering) and dealing with our feelings, beliefs, values, acts, and attitudes as we move through life with an SMI loved one. Sample strategies include:

*   Finding new meaning in our situation
*   Working
*   Developing emotional mobility
*   Outgrowing the "Why me?" syndrome
*   Practicing altruism
*   Mastering *sadhana*

Finding new meaning involves developing a philosophy of life that fits well for us in our various situations. As Victor Frankl wrote in 1946, after his horrendous World War II concentration camp experiences, "We must never forget that we may also find meaning in life when confronted with a hopeless situation, when facing a fate that cannot be changed."

So what meaning exists in dealing with SMI? In the past fifty years, many of us in the United States have grown up trying to solve problems by using tools such as the scientific method or psychological insight. These are good when they work, but all the empirical data or insight in the world does not ease the pain of watching a loved one suffer. So how else can we approach problems or create meaning for ourselves?

Many philosophies exist and may be worth exploring. You may want to adapt ideas or tools from several sources. For some, religion is deeply comforting. The point is, as Frankl also wrote, that one uniquely human capacity is our ability to "transform a personal tragedy into a triumph, to turn one's predicament into a human achievement" (p. 135). In some ways, this is what some of us have done by joining the Alliance for the Mentally Ill. We cannot change the fact of mental illness, but we can achieve other things for mentally ill people and for ourselves.

Weisman also commented on this in his 1984 book, *The Coping Capacity*: "Our one obligation to cope well enough to make survival significant is about all we can be sure about" (p. 157). This simple statement is an example of how philosophy can help clarify our priorities, especially when events unnerve and confuse us.

Working can be another coping behavior. Freud once said: "Work is the closest thing to sanity." Finding meaningful work or activities, or both, is one of the best strategies for nourishing ourselves. Life holds more than the mental illness of our loved ones. The curative value of recreation and fun, distraction, and work should never be underestimated. Some people find that the awesome power of the wilderness helps them keep problems in perspective. Physical exercise helps others. If it works, use it!

Developing emotional mobility may be a first step toward freeing ourselves for meaningful activity. In 1985, three researchers from the field of gerontology (Cantor, Jarret, and Brody) each studied family caregivers of frail elderly people. Many of these elders also had brain disabilities in the form of dementias. The three studies discovered that the most important and consistent factor among high-coping caregivers was their ability to distance themselves emotionally from their loved one. This enabled them to do what needed doing.

What works for caregivers of the elderly may not work for us. Then again, it may. The dynamic seems the same. Much needs to be done for the frail elderly, and relatives who are chronically overwhelmed by grief, resentment, and a host of other emotions would not have energy left for providing the needed care. Getting some emotional distance leaves them more energy for caregiving, for doing the job.

The same may apply to our situation, but distancing ourselves is easier suggested than done. Our culture emphasizes undying familial love, so distancing from our loved ones may feel wrong. But chances are that it is a helpful mechanism for coping.

Outgrowing the "Why me?" syndrome also takes awhile. Feeling that we are being singled out for suffering is a natural reaction to loss, initially, and people move through this reaction at various rates.

Down the road a minute or a mile, we can then expand our perspective and move out of our isolated grief. Conservative estimates are that one family out of four deals with equally great stresses and heartaches—such as those arising from tragic physical disabilities, substance abuse or addiction, the death of a child, and so on. (I do not offer this comparison to reduce our burden or discount our feelings. It just helps to know that we have counterparts. Misery loves company.)

Additionally, according to the federal government's 1980 national plan for research on child and adolescent disorders, at least 12 percent of children under eighteen have a mental disorder, and half of these 7,500,000 children are severely handicapped by their disorders (Peschel & Peschel, 1992). That's one out of eight children. This rough statistic can help us understand that we are not being singled out.

Practicing altruism emerges in many people who cope with severe hardship. Helping others in even greater need can be therapeutic, and it has the big advantage of helping both ourselves and others. A few years ago, for instance, the grieving parents and family of Debra Beebe donated large sums of money to the University of Wisconsin, where their daughter had once been a graduate student at the School of Social Work. Shortly after starting her career as a social worker, Debra had been killed by a man who was mentally ill. Her parents wanted their money to help other students training to work with SMI.

All of us who were affected marveled at their strength and generosity. In turn, we showed them affection and admiration for their altruism, which probably was comforting and healing for these parents. In all likelihood, their way of coping was healthier for them than suing someone, and it surely is wonderful for those students who benefit from their kindness and financial support.

Mastering sadhana refers to a Sanskrit word meaning "spirituality." This idea came from Valles (1988), who went on extensive retreats with Anthony De Mello, a spiritual director. Valles then wrote about mastering sadhana, advising (p. 38):

> Don't fret about things. Things are what they are, and life is what it is. . . . If you rebel and protest, you are the loser. . . . You are hitting your head against a wall, you are hurting yourself with the hard rock of reality. But if you understand and accept reality as it is, you get in tune with life, you enter the current, you ride the storm.

To soften its impact, most of us pad ourselves against the "hard rock" of reality. We protect ourselves through our own model of the world, which we develop in the context of our traditions, training, and the customs of our family and culture. This model is in some sense arbitrary—nowhere is it written in stone. Some of our reaction, then, comes from our inner conditioning, which tells us that we must do something to alleviate the suffering and to make things better. Valles (1988) exemplified this notion by pointing out that a married man in India would be very upset if a guest in his house slept with his wife, but an Eskimo man might invite a guest to do so. The point is that part of our upset comes not from outside causes (e.g., the mental illness of our loved one), but rather from inside— from our minds, which have been conditioned to view the mental illness as catastrophic. To paraphrase it in the words of *sadhana*: "Nobody upsets you; you upset yourself."

Perhaps some of us can change or modify that part of the conditioning that is hurting us. We may benefit from exploring the coping strategies used by eastern civilization, by different American Indian tribes, and so on. This is a big world we live in; all human beings have struggled with tragedy and coping. Many systems of thought exist other than the ones mentioned in this book. Explore them and use anything that works for you.

Professional Help

Are there times when professional help is in order? If we could afford the time and money, it might be wonderful to tell all our troubles to a willing and knowledgeable professional. We do not have to be neurotic, weak, or troubled to benefit from counseling or other professional help. Loving a relative who has severe mental illness is a tough burden to carry alone, so any and all help can be useful.

Most of us can manage within our own resources, and we can find invaluable emotional and educational support through NAMI and AMI groups. Meanwhile, some specific signs indicate the possible need for profesisonal help:

- Feeling very bad too often. How much is "too often"? Again, no formula fits everyone, so use your own judgment.
- Feeling absolutely stuck in the pain and unable to handle it.
- Facing too many crises all at once, and knowing that your reserve tank is drained. Insomnia, weight fluctuation, severe depression, anxiety, fatigue—these all are symptoms of running out of reserves.
- Feeling that problems are "unspeakable."
- Needing education about the illnesses and treatments, coping/ management skills, or resources in your community.
- Feeling devastated by loss for an extended period.

Preventing severe emotional breakdown is easier than altering it once it has occurred. Professional help may be the best route to go at times. For instance, grief counseling does help some people. Counselors can help us avoid the risk of losing the support of friends and family by overtaxing them with too much talk about our grief. But it is essential that counselors recognize grief and respond to it in such a way as to validate and normalize the experience for families.

Coping with Grief

As discussed in chapter 7, it is important to distinguish grief caused by SMI in the family from other griefs. We have all seen people who latch on to a particular kind of grief to explain all situations. Doing this puts us at risk for getting stuck in a morass of problems that we could otherwise resolve.

Having suffered severe early loss (e.g., the death of a parent, or a serious childhood illness) puts people at increased risk for reacting strongly to future losses. If this is your case, professional help might make things easier for you.

Feelings of being alone and abandoned in our grief are hard to take. Knowing others who are coping with similar grief can be very comforting, but most of the hours of our lives are spent among people who do not truly understand. One of my dearest friends once said, in trying to help me about my son: "Please try not to catastrophize the next time David goes into the hospital. Your panic runs amuck, and you make things worse for yourself."

She was, and is, absolutely right, and I knew it even at the time she was saying it. But I snapped back, "Don't you presume to tell me how to feel or act. You can't begin to understand this pain." I bet she will not try to comfort me again, either, which will be even worse.

When people ask: "How is David?", I'm usually pleased. But sometimes a sarcastic response jumps to mind: "Still schizophrenic." I do not say that out loud. Instead, I respond with what feel like empty sentences: "He's the same [better/worse]." I sometimes go into detail; often I cry. And every time, I wonder why I am utterly unable to communicate the mystery of which I have become a part.

Surely nothing is to be gained in such behavior, as it puts everyone involved in a no-win situation. So what if a good friend or relative cannot really understand? We have to accept and be grateful for attempts at understanding, for compassion and caring, and for asking. Second best is better than nothing, we need to learn, like it or not.

Intense grief is an unwelcome companion, and anyone who willingly enters into the pain of another is an unusual person. Some people do this professionally, but that is different from the intense, continual involvement of a close friend or relative. Most of us do fairly well by our friends in a crisis, for a short time. But sharing the ongoing grief that accompanies SMI may be asking too much from our friends. We risk alienating people, and in the long run we end up even lonelier. So we do need to watch how often, and to whom, we release our full-blown grief.

Creative Writers on Coping

When upset, we first listen to the voices of professional authorities whom we think have some answers to our questions. Sometimes this helps, but the plot thickens as we discover that the world has a multitude of authorities to offer us adivce and solutions. Often we end up quite confused.

Creative writers, in all their subjective glory, sometimes speak in clearer tones. Feldman and Kornfield (1991) have crafted such clarity in their book *Stories of the Spirit, Stories of the Heart,* and the rest of this section draws entirely on their work. I present a few gems for your consideration or rejection, whichever suits you best. From page 8:

> No other person can tell us exactly how to
> live our life, no matter how wise or loving that
> person is. No one has ever lived our life before.

We ourselves must learn how to live with
integrity and wisdom.

Then, from their section on "The Triumph of the Human Heart"
(p. 170):

> In even the worst landscapes of human dark-
> ness and difficulty there shine beams of light.
> They are not necessarily cast by particularly
> powerful or holy people who possess gran-
> diose strategies for changing the world. They
> most often radiate from simple, ordinary
> people who in their ultimate encounters with
> tragedy, injustice, and terror have been trans-
> formed and have learned how to respond to
> the world around them. . . . Through their
> example our eyes are opened to the possi-
> bilities of bringing light to our own shadows.

This surely has been my observation over years of talking with
family members, students, and people who have an SMI. It is not
always clear to me how these people managed to overcome their
tragedies and griefs, but it is clear that for large periods of time, they
have done so. It does not happen overnight, so do not despair if you
presently are under shadows.

Human beings have an amazing capacity for self-
awareness. It allows us to make choices and to learn and grow
through life's tragedies rather than being overwhelmed by them.
The next page in *Stories of the Spirit* reads:

> The gift of our awareness means that we
> need not be driven by instincts of protective-
> ness and hostility but instead that we can
> carefully nurture our capacities for forgive-
> ness and understanding.

Sweet words.

What Is the Answer?

The more one reads, in both the social sciences and the creative writers, the more one sees that no single authority holds *the* answer. No one else can travel or find the path for us. As the wonderful old song goes, "We have to walk that lonesome valley by ourselves."

Nonetheless, the spiritual quest to overcome grief has been made by generations of people from all walks of life, and from all cultures. We can take some comfort in knowing we are not alone. We can explore the wisdom of other cultures and understand that we are not so much in need of experts as to define our own ways of knowing and coping. Then we can understand something of what rages and grief we need to let go of in order to embrace some of the beauties and joys available to us. Or, as Chassid wrote (Feldman & Kornfield, p. 238):

> A rabbi was always teaching his followers to seek the answers in themselves. But the followers always came back expecting more answers from him.
>
> Finally he set up a booth with a sign: "Any two questions answered for $100."
>
> After some deliberation, one of his richest followers decided to ask, and brought two important questions. He paid the money and said as he did, "Isn't $100 rather costly for just two questions?"
>
> "Yes," said the rabbi, "and what is your second question?"

Clinical Implications

Potok (1980, p. 265), an artist who went blind, urged student-clinicians at the Boston University Medical School

> not to judge their future patients harshly and to understand that people's response to life-

> threatening or way-of-life–threatening events
> is unpredictable, especially in the face of the
> wanton promises of miracles from science
> and medicine.

His words apply as much to mental illness as to blindness. The SMI scene also includes unpredictable responses (e.g., the kind of grief that accompanies these illnesses) and wanton promises of miracles (e.g., megavitamins, kidney dialysis, new drugs). Clinicians: be patient, and not too quick to judge and label your clients and client families.

Other implications include the following clinical aims.

- Help people consider the idea that life can be good in spite of feeling bad more often than they would like.
- Educate and help people stop blaming themselves for SMI; help them reassess their guilt and its underlying assumptions or beliefs.
- Help people distinguish what they can influence, what they can control, and what is beyond influence or control.
- Help people add to their repertoire for coping: assess/reinforce what's already in the repertoire, and identify options that could be added (see Greenley's list, earlier in this chapter).
- Help people value themselves for their roles and their growth during the process of coping.
- Help people connect with local resources and AMI group(s).
- Help people express their anger and add to their repertoire for expressing it constructively.
- Help families develop crisis-management strategies.
- Learn more about SMI grief and normalize it for clients.
- Reinforce emotional mobility.
- Work to avoid burnout for self as well as clients.

Summary

Many families have members who are severely disabled in one way or another. Families that deal with severe mental illness have not been singled out for suffering. Our mentally ill relatives have it worse than we do. We need to develop a philosophy of life that works for us and helps us find meaning. People who can think flexibly, who can reshape their ideas and feelings from multiple perspectives, have an advantage over people who are rigid in their thinking. We also need to increase our coping capacities just as much as we can. Paradoxically, it is equally important to accept our human limitations.

It is very important to move beyond "If only I had . . ." and to accept the inevitability of sadness, anger, and grief without inflicting on ourselves some notion that we should not have negative feelings. Dealing with mental illness is a part of our lives, but we do not need to let it take over. There are many other things to life.

To come to terms with strong negative feelings, we need to find some balance between knowing the world is neither safe and predictable nor entirely dangerous. Events can still make sense, but not always; we are decent and competent people, and helplessness is also one of our feelings.

The survivor who recovers from loss sometimes sees trauma as a potential source of strength and victory. If not victory over the event, it may at least be victory by enduring. How often we hear someone say with pride: "I survived!" Many people speak of a renewed appreciation of the good in life, after they know how bad things can be. Wisdom of maturity replaces the ignorance of naivete. The survivor emerges somewhat sadder but considerably wiser.

In the end, families hope for the best. This acknowledges the real possibilities, both good and bad, of disasters and triumphs, in spite of our human limitations to control.

References

Brody, E. M. (1985). Parent care as a normative family stress. *The Gerontologist, 25*(1), 19–29.

Bulman, R. J. (1992). *Shattered assumptions*. New York: The Free Press.

Cantor, M. (1983). Strain among caregivers: A study of experience in the U. S. *The Gerontologist, 23*(6), 597–604.

Feldman, C., & Kornfield, J. (Eds.). (1991). *Stories of the spirit, stories of the heart: Parables of the spiritual path from around the world.* San Francisco: Harper.

Frankl, V. (1946). *Man's search for meaning.* New York: Washington Square Press.

Greenley, J., McKee, D., Stein, L., Griffin-Francell, C., & Greenberg, J. (1989, Aug.). Families coping with schizophrenia: Stress and distress. Paper presented at the meeting of the Society for the Study of Social Problems, Berkeley, CA

Jarret, W. H. (1985). Caregiving within kinship systems: Is affection really necessary? *The Gerontologist, 25*(1), 5–10.

MacGregor, P. (1984). Grief: The unrecognized parental response to mental illness in a child. *Social Work, 39*(2), 160–166.

Peschel, R. E., & Peschel, E. (1992, Fall). Neurobiological disorders in children and adolescents: A scientific approach. *Innovations and Research, 4,* 15–19.

Valles, S. J. C. (1988). *Mastering sadhana: On retreat with Anthony De Mello.* Garden City, NY: Doubleday.

Weisman, A. (1984). *The coping capacity.* New York: Human Sciences Press.

X

PROCESS:

Spiraling in and Out

Grief, coping, and control are all linked together in one big whirling process. Much as we like to think of ourselves as progressing in a straight line from one point to another, that is not how most of us function. Even under ideal circumstnces, we weave in and out, up and down, with good days and bad days. Living with severe mental illness in our midst is more like being caught in the eye of a hurricane.

We each try to come to grips with this process, and a variety of disciplines have different beliefs about the best way for people to handle long-term stress. Various religions offer solutions with an emphasis on faith, prayer, and moral behavior. Various psychotherapies offer solutions; some emphasize insight into the unconscious workings of the mind, others emphasize cognitive restructuring, rational emotive therapy, and so forth. Most of these beliefs overlap, but each discipline tends to emphasize one aspect more than another or give a different slant to its interpretation. For this reason, I present several views on the lengthy process of coping, so you can select what makes the most sense to you.

Spirals of Coping

Schuchardt (1989) studied 500 biographies of handicapped people and their families, to look at what she called an
eight-stage process of coping. The handicaps included mental
illness, cancer, multiple sclerosis, epilepsy, and a few other physical
disabilities. Mental illnesses were the most commonly studied. She
purposely used the term *spirals of coping* because she found that,
while at least a third of these people often got stuck in the initial
stages and another third in transitional stages, almost everyone
spiraled back and forth between stages. Schuchardt emphasized
the incompleteness of internal coping processes. People seldom
progress smoothly, but rather spin in and out of the following
stages:

1. *Uncertainty.* The initial reaction to tragedy is usually shock.
    Lightning strikes and destroys the order and expectations of
    our lives. Panic and anxiety set in. We cannot bear the un-
    known and fight to resist it. Confusion, denial, and an inability
    to take it all in are common first reactions. This can be called a
    phase of entry or recognition. It often involves ignorance
    ("What does *mental illness* mean?"), insecurity ("It must mean
    something, but what?"), and an inability to accept the news ("It
    must be a mistake").

2. *Certainty.* The next phase often is expressed in the form of
    "Yes, this is a serious illness, but surely it cannot be in my
    family." It is possible to experience an affirmation and a con-
    tinuation of the denial at the same time. As Schuchardt says,
    "Even those who have recognized their crises have to deny it
    time and time again in order to be able to go on living" (p. 66).
    The ambivalent "yes, but" reaction often reflects our need to
    buy time so that we do not collapse.

3. *Displaced aggression.* At this point, people are shattered to
    their very core. They may lash out at others or withdraw. The

tough part is that the object of the tragedy and aggression cannot be grasped or attacked. How do you attack a mental illness? So we tend to unload our aggression in all directions, against anything and everything. Some people fall into an apathetic resignation or sink into a morass of isolation.

4. *Negotiation and bargaining.* At this part of the spiral, we will do anything to escape our sense of impotence in the face of what looks like a hopeless situation. Here begins the endless search for doctors and treatment; answers to why it happened; and for some people, a search for miracle cures: megavitamins, primal screams, psychotherapy, reparenting—you name it, we'll try it. History is replete with such attempts: pilgrimages to Lourdes, the saying of masses, the laying on of hands, making vows, and so forth.

5. *Depression.* Sooner or later, we see that all of our attempts to negotiate and bargain have failed. "Emotions directed outwards are spent and have given way to a burial of hope directed inwards" (p. 69). It all seems useless and meaningless. Common to this depression is an abandonment of unrealistic hopes. This very painful "burial of hope" is accompanied by an infinite sorrow, and we move inward to an encounter with ourselves. Giving up our unrealistic hopes has its positive side as well, in that we stop searching for impossible cures.

6. *Acceptance.* This phase of the spiral entails the intense mourning of past, present, and future. The beloved person of the past has changed beyond recognition, the present is terrible, and the future looks grim. We come to what feels like an end, and we are exhausted. However, we may also recognize that we are still alive, and not alone. This is a turning point for some of us. Thoughts of "I can . . . I will . . . I am" come to mind between bouts of mourning.

7. *Activity.* Acceptance releases powers which hitherto we spent in fighting and depression. What now becomes key is not what we have but what we make of it ("If life gives you a lemon, make lemonade"). Many people rechannel their energy into the National Alliance for the Mentally Ill, into working or volunteering in mental health centers, or into political and advocacy activities.

8. *Solidarity.* When they join with others to fight and advocate for their common cause, people experience solidarity. (Not everyone has the time, energy, or capacity for this phase of coping.)

In looking over this list, it is easy to see why Schuchardt referred to spirals. Which of us has not spiraled in and out dozens of times? Tidy and neat it is not.

Forgiveness and Coping

Flanigan, in her book *Forgiving the Unforgivable* (1992), wrote about the need to *name* the unforgivable. That is, what precisely is it that we find unforgivable? Is it the bad genes? The fact that we could not protect our loved ones? That we find no help and no cure? That others in the family abandoned the ill person and/or us? Is it the illness itself? Flanigan emphasized the complexities and importance of being able to identify and name the unforgivable. This may take time and effort.

Stage two of Flanigan's theory involved understanding that we did the best we know how, given our particular set of circumstances. So many factors enter here, including:

Our level of knowledge about serious mental illnesses
Support or lack thereof from family, health care, and legal systems

Our level of pain and fear
Our health
Economic resources
Other children in the family
The culture and era in which we live

Next, Flanigan mentioned the value of accepting that "bad things happen to good people," and that life is neither fair nor predictable. Acceptance also involves facing that there is no cure, and that we are powerless over the illness. This one is particularly confusing, because we do have some power over our behavior and actions, which can affect the illness. The trick is not to confuse this with cure.

Then it is important to know that our relative did not choose to be ill. This can be hard to grasp in the beginning stages of a mental illness, when nobody knows what is going on. After we get a diagnosis and then learn a lot about SMI, it becomes clear for most of us. No one chooses to be mentally ill. The complication is that this is not yet clear to our culture. Most people are ignorant about SMI and do blame both the ill people and their families.

Flanigan wrote about our capacity to transform personal tragedy into human achievement and meaning. And last, but surely not least (maybe most!), is our capacity to feel that we deserve our own lives and satisfactions, separate from those of our ill relative.

Flanigan based her findings on her interviews with people who had suffered a grievous loss. Some people managed to survive their losses rather well, in terms of moving on with their lives. Others seemed unable to forgive the person or thing that had done them harm. Some of the long-term processes that Flanigan described seemed to apply to the process of coping with SMI in the family. It can be a long, arduous struggle from "Why did this happen to me?" to "That's life, and we have to make the best of it."

Burnout

Rediger (1982), a clergyman, wrote about coping with clergy burnout. People of faith have been very active in housing and feeding homeless people, of whom approximately one-third are estimated to be mentally ill. *Burnout* is the exhaustion of physical, emotional, and spiritual resources. Rediger said the maximum emotional survival span for clergy doing intensive community organization work is about three years. Since those of us working and living with SMI are also involved in very intensive work, this raises vital questions.

The most energy-draining pressure point lies in any significant discrepancy between expectation and reality. For SMI people, family members, and clinicians, it is a struggle to set reasonable expectations. We don't want to set our standards so low that the person with SMI does nothing; nor do we want to set our expectations so high that, once again, nothing is achieved. Our SMI relative may be harmed at either extreme. Meanwhile, however, we drain ourselves as we search for the realistic part of the spectrum. This is no one's fault; dividing attainable goals from the unattainable is very hard. Even if we get a good feel for reality at a certain time, it may totally change the next week, if not the next hour! So we do not always know what expectations to have. We keep trying, and eventually we burn out.

Rediger described both the emotional and physical characteristics of burnout in terms of three stages:

1. Early stage: increasing irritability, whining and complaining about things
2. Middle stage: trying even harder, worrying, sporadic efforts, and mood swings
3. Advanced stage: intolerance, hostility, cynicism, apathy, insomnia, becoming less effective at problem solving, and loss of sense of humor

In terms of physical health, burnout manifests in low energy, exhausted appearance, frequent headaches, and sometimes gastric upsets. In terms of spirituality, Rediger pointed to loss of faith in self and the system, one-track thinking, becoming judgmental of self and others, and listlessness.

Our culture emphasizes the work ethic, Rediger said, which assumes that any task or goal can be accomplished if we just try hard enough. But he suggested we try *smarter,* not harder.

> When I keep banging my nose up against the same stone wall, I can continue doing that and get used to the taste of my own blood, or I can run away, or I can back off and start observing the situation and ask myself sensible questions about the stone wall and my relationship to it.

Good words!

Another concept emphasized more in the religious realm than the secular is learning to suffer. We can try to get rid of suffering, try to bear it, or try to integrate it. All three approaches are part of mourning and coping, and perhaps we have to ask ourselves a few questions here:

- Which part of our pain can we get rid of? Can we rid ourselves of unrealistic expectations, for example? Or of blaming ourselves for something we did or did not do?
- What can we bear? The notion that there is no cure at this time? That bad things do happen to good people?
- What parts of all this do we try to integrate into our lives? For example, if he is my brother, do I simply accept that I will see him once a month, like it or not? Or that I will feel a period of sadness from time to time, no matter what I try to do to avoid it?

In other words, we can learn to suffer with style.

Unhelpful Responses to Stress

Wishful thinking and attempting to undo what has happened is a no-win game. "If only I had . . ." seldom works. People often become drawn into fantasies about what might have happened if only they had handled things differently. The obvious drawback is that no amount of longing alters what has already happened. Whether or not we could have done things differently, the mental illness likely could not have been prevented.

Another destructive response to pain is to use drugs or alcohol. Some people under stress consume too much alcohol, caffeine, or nicotine, too many painkillers, tranquilizers, sleeping pills, or antidepressants. The short-term use of antidepressants, sleeping pills, or tranquilizers can put a floor under a terrible crisis, of course, thereby preventing further deterioration. But all these drugs interfere with the biochemistry of emotions, and may even delay new learning and healing. Caffeine, for example, produces anxiety symptoms if used in excess. Sleeping pills eventually disturb sleep. And alcohol is a depressant.

Some people cope with their pain by destructive eating patterns. Siblings and children with mentally ill parents sometimes act out and cause trouble at home or school. Other people become compulsive in their work habits. There are no end of possibilities.

Many of us use repression and distraction to try to avoid pain. These buy us time while we begin the process of reconstructing our inner world. Keeping busy doing things, so that we concentrate on the task at hand rather than painful feelings, can certainly be a useful coping technique. If used to excess, however, it can be dysfunctional: some people end up living in a sort of numbed-out fog if they rely on repression and distraction too much. The other problem is that repressing pain by distracting ourselves often does not work very well. How much is "too much"? Who knows? No formula here either. Ideally, we each reach a point where we can experience and tolerate our feelings, at least for a while. We need to feel the desolation of loss, and we need to know that it will not kill us.

Giving ourselves negative messages under stress does not help. I am referring to such thoughts as: "I won't be able to get through this. I'm going mad. This is terrible; my life is ruined. I'll never be happy again. No one understands how awful I feel; I'm completely alone. Something even worse is going to happen. There is no point of going on. This is going to make me really ill."

There is no point in pretending that we can or should will away negative thoughts, but they do not enhance our well-being. Sometimes we do need to "say it out loud" (as chapter 8 describes). The point is that, while we all have dark thoughts, we need to move from telling ourselves "I can't do anything" to "I am doing the best I can right now, and I don't have to be perfect."

Helpful Responses

We do have ways of opening up options for ourselves. Here are some common strategies for coping with the stresses and pain of SMI in the family.

- Seek information and guidance.
- Share concerns and find consolation by talking with sympathetic people.
- To get some rest, put the problem(s) out of your mind for a while, by whatever (non–self-destructive) means necessary.
- Keep busy with activities you enjoy.
- Review alternatives and examine consequences.
- Face what you are feeling in your own way, e.g., by keeping a stiff upper lip or by "letting it all hang out."

This list is full of contradictions. But the research—and experience—say that those of us who cope well tend to use a wider range of strategies, specializing in the ones we know best. Thus, we do well to try out new strategies when our old ones are not working.

It is important to do what is possible. If we try new approaches and they fail, we do not need to catastrophize ("Nothing works"). We do not need to punish ourselves or anyone else. Rather, we can ask: "What can be done new?" Keeping a certain degree of composure helps. (I am talking about an even-tempered caution, not an artificial serenity.) If we can cultivate some self-confidence along the way, that also helps.

This chapter is beginning to sound like a cooking recipe! Try a pinch of composure and two ounces of caution, spread generously with self-confidence, and bake until "smarter, not harder."

Magic solutions or absolutes do not work with burnout and stress. Solutions, even when we do find them, are seldom permanent. Coping really is an endless spiraling process. Try not to shoulder all the responsibility alone. If you have good friends, relatives, or trusted professionals, use them when you need them.

Tragedy happens, and we seldom have the control over it that we would like. So the best we can do is to revise and redefine our coping skills, keep the faith, and keep on trucking. We can develop a healthy respect for our limitations and a trust in being able to survive. As that wonderful grandmother said in chapter 5, "It could have been worse."

References

Flanigan, B. (1992). *Forgiving the unforgivable*. New York: Macmillan.

MacGregor, P. (1994). Grief: The unrecognized parental response to mental illness in a child. *Social Work, 39*(2), 160–166.

Rediger, G. (1982). *Coping with clergy burnout*. Valley Forge, PA: Judson Press.

Schuchardt, E. (1989). *Coping with failure: "Why Me?": Opportunities for learning to live* (pp. 58–79). [I ran across this book in a Benedictine Retreat library in Middleton, Wisconsin, in 1992. When I went back to get the name of its publisher, the book was nowhere to be found; and a computer search was also unsuccessful. My recollection is that this was a short book dealing with clergy burnout. I obviously considered it a good and relevant resource. My apologies for losing the citation.]

XI

HOPE

Hope is an important human emotion and coping mechanism, especially when dealing with devastating mental illness. Both a belief and an emotion, it is very private for most people. For people with SMI, for instance, revealing their hopes means exposing themselves to vulnerability and feelings of shame. They have already had their hopes dashed to the ground repeatedly.

People suffering with SMI tend to view the future differently than do their family members, so understanding hope's role may prove helpful. Professionals also vary in their hopes for each SMI client, depending on their beliefs about the illness's etiology and treatment, as well as their respective personalities.

To better understand these differing hopes, I organized a study in 1989 by some skilled, experienced, and sensitive graduate students in social work who were majoring in SMI. Data was also gathered by social workers in Michigan. In all, they interviewed fifty parents, fifty clients with diagnoses of SMI (half of whom lived in the community, half in mental hospitals), and fifty professionals who work with SMI adults. First, the interviewer read the following definitions of hope: "to cherish a desire with expectation of fulfillment; something that is desired; to long for and expect to get something." The student or social worker usually elaborated until he or she felt that the person understood how we wanted to use the word.

Then came the open question, "What do you feel about *hope* for yourself [your child/your client]? Since we cannot assess hope directly, our findings are based on what these people said, or seemed to be saying. In other words, we listened for inferences and drew deductions.

This method for "measuring" hope is not perfect: it assumes that people are aware of their hopes, express them without distorting them, and do not fluctuate in their feelings and hopes from one instant to the next. None of these assumptions always holds true for anyone, let alone for people living with SMI, who may feel ashamed of the illness.

Even with these limitations, however, our findings were illuminating. Blending information from our study and from the literature, the following sections discuss the hopes of adults with SMI, parents of people with SMI, and professionals who work with people with SMI.

Hope in Adults with SMI

For most people living with SMI, life is a painful nightmare and an unending struggle. If one theme resounds among the severely mentally ill, it is the wish to be normal.

Interviewer: Did anything special happen over New Year's?
Subject: Yes. A man in the store asked me for a match—just as if I were a person.

All our interviews and all the literature by clients reported the express desire to be "normal" and to be accepted as such by others.

People's hopes for "normal" lives often seemed to include a desire for control over their lives and for acceptance by their families and friends. Those interviewees who were in locked wards and had little or no contact with their families frequently said they had no hope. These people have little control over their lives and often feel rejected by their relatives and friends. Society's low expectations for such people in the areas of employment, independent living, marriage, children, and health were reflected in our subjects' hopes.

Of the people we interviewed, few mentioned wanting marriage and a family. They did not seem to consider these realistic goals. Many expressed a desire for acceptance. One woman, age forty, simply said she wanted to be accepted by her father. Another complained that people rarely talk to her, and she said she has nowhere to go. She is seventy-eight. People we interviewed were acutely aware of societal stigma against them.

Asking about hope is a very personal question, one that many people with SMI avoid thinking about. It requires them to evaluate their current situation and assess realistic expectations. Unfortunately, what many of our subjects considered realistic for themselves was not what they wanted in their futures. In some cases, this seemed too painful to contemplate, and we got some strong reactions. As a twenty-six-year-old male said, "I don't know what I'll be doing ten years from now. I have a hard time thinking about what I'll be doing tomorrow—I don't want to answer that question. I don't feel all that hopeful right now."

When they did dare look into the future, many people denied having any hope: "I know what it feels like not to have any hope," said a twenty-eight-year-old man. "When I was locked up and had 3500 milligrams of Thorazine in me, I had no hope." This reminded me of a poem by someone who has schizophrenia:

> Nowhere to go
> Nothing to do
> Worthless paces
> Hopeless thoughts
> Ravaged faces
> Nuclear blast
> Death at last.
> —from *The Lighthouse* (1987)

Some people hoped for better mental health. As one man put it, "I wish it [schizophrenia] would just go away by itself." One woman hoped that new medications would be discovered that would change the way she feels. In general, people were not optimistic: "I hope to get rid of these voices, but I don't think I ever will," said a man in his early thirties.

Close to half of our interviewees with SMI expressed hopes of being gainfully employed. However, they often tempered their hopes with the reality of their situations: "I hope to get a job at a television station. . . . I don't know when this will happen. I really don't even know if it will, but I hope so."

Findings from our study parallel those in Godschalx's (1987) doctoral dissertation on the experiences and coping strategies of people with schizophrenia. Her study included fifteen males and fifteen females between the ages of twenty-one and thirty-five. She found three major dimensions to their hopes: seeking security, managing emotional pain, and finding meaning. "Seeking security" involved a search for psychological, physical, economic, and interpersonal security. We interpreted similar findings to be a search for control over one's life and acceptance by others.

"Managing emotional pain" referred to the pain of general functioning. Godschalx attributed this emotional pain to a loss of ability and a loss of normality. We, too, saw people trying to manage their emotional pain, and we also attributed the pain to a loss of normality. People seemed to look for more control and acceptance as ways of managing this pain.

"Finding meaning" was a search for a role or activity that provided a sense of usefulness. We saw this as a search for normality, which was manifested in a search for control and acceptance. People who were functioning at a higher level than average also expressed hopes for getting more control over their lives. Expressions of hope were more commonly seen in post- or never-institutionalized people. Dashed dreams and despair, however, were the most common themes; and when someone with SMI had lost all hope, it seemed that apathy set in.

Godschalx found eight major coping strategies: to ignore it and live, to work at getting better, to adopt the attitude of: "See, everybody has problems," to hope the future will be better, to believe it's over, to question the situation, to resign self to illness, and to view the situation alternatively. Of these strategies, Godschalx believed that three provided hope: working at getting better, realizing that everybody has problems, and hoping the future will be better. The similarities between Godschalx's findings and ours reinforce our ideas about the hopes of people with SMI.

HOPE AS AFFECTED BY DEINSTITUTIONALIZATION

We wondered whether and how deinstitutionalization had affected hope in people with mental illnesses. To this end, we divided the literature by clients into materials written prior to 1955, and after 1970. The fifteen-year gap was designed to reduce the likelihood of people writing from a reference point that encompassed both eras.

Writers in the institutionalization era (e.g., Gregory, 1952; King, 1964; Sinnett, 1964) were more often inclined to put their hopes for the future in an abstract religious power than were persons in the post-deinstitutionalization era. Those in the latter group (e.g., Vonnegut, 1975; Worth, 1987; Folkard, 1992; Brown, 1993) were far more likely to emphasize optimism regarding the shift from a psychodynamic basis for understanding SMI toward a more biological model.

The areas most frequently mentioned as sources of despair were involuntary hospitalization and being subjected to treatment modalities that clients felt were useless or harmful. Electroconvulsive therapy was the most frequently mentioned treatment despised by persons prior to 1955; after 1970, the most frequent complaint was the side effects of psychotropic medications.

A few more generalizations were gleaned from the literature, pre- and post-deinstitutionalization. Prior to 1955, patients seemed overwhelmed with feelings of failure and they expressed very little hope. After 1970, patients cited improved medications as a source of hope, hope for making it in the community, and even hope for being "normal" one day. People in the era after deinstitutionalization expressed less despair.

The present suicide rate among males with schizophrenia is estimated at 10 percent in the United States. In talking with and reading about the despair and lack of hope that many seem to feel, we wonder at their bravery to survive at all. Hope seems to be a key issue. Those who still have some hope express a willingness to struggle for survival. And those people who seem to have lost hope express a sort of pervasive numbness. We are not surprised at the suicide rate, but rather admire those who continue to struggle in the face of diminishing hopes.

Parents' Perspectives

In our sample of fifty parents, only five were fathers, so our findings slant toward mothers' perspectives. We know much less about fathers. Our sample of parents ranged in age from forty to seventy-one, with the majority being in their late fifties. How long their adult children had been ill ranged from five years to the child's entire life. All our interviews were done with Midwestern middle-class white parents. We surely have not learned the definitive parental perspectives on hope, but certain themes did emerge irrespective of age, number of years of coping, and economic and social supports. Moreover, these themes were very similar to those in the literature written by family members (e.g., Wilson, 1968; Deveson, 1991; Backlar, 1994).

Parents' hopes for their children ran the whole gamut, from despair to high hopes. Many parents expressed hope that scientific research in the "hard" sciences would turn up a cure for SMI or at least more effective medications.

There did seem to be an understandable conflict between maintaining and giving up hope. Parents are caught in a painful double bind: giving up hope for their child's having a normal good life is painful, yet some parents need to relinquish a large measure of hope before they can successfully get on with their own lives.

At one end of the vast continuum of feelings about this bind is the story Moorman (1992, p. 30) wrote about trying to help her mother give up hope for a cure for her daughter with SMI:

> "If I felt like you, Peggy, I'd kill myself,"
> Mother would answer. And she did in a way.
> As she began to accept Sally's disability, her
> own natural resilience against gloom failed
> her. In just a few years she was beaten, de-
> feated, exhausted. And then she died.

At the other end of the spectrum is the mother who said: "He has taught us about courage, and in the struggle to understand

and to help, we have all become the stronger and better for it." We also heard everything in between. With or without hope, haunting tones of sadness were always present, expressing an overriding concern for their children's suffering.

Another theme was despair because the illnesses have no cures, the treatments are devastating, community resources are few and inadequate, and both the mental health and legal systems are often unresponsive. Lack of clarity around SMI's process and outcomes means that many parents cycle through hope and despair. As Spaniol et al. (1993) point out, this is a *normal* reaction. Both hope and expectations fall as the years of coping go by. We heard:

> "Over a fifteen-year period, we have gone from the totally unrealistic hope for a total cure based on our ignorance and denial, to total despair based on knowledge about the disease and the severe form of it our son has. Now I have no hope left—which enables me to get on with my life, but is the ultimate sadness."

and

> "The more I learned about SMI . . . the more my hopes gave way to despair."

A sad but significant twist exists here. It seems that the more parents understand and learn about SMI, the better they become at coping and the more they give up certain kinds of hope. To go on, some parents have to give up hope for their children's recovery. In the heartbreaking words of a mother:

> "As his hopes and dreams have died along with ours, I still find it difficult to give up hope completely. For without a little hope in my heart, the pain would be unbearable. And yet, I have no hope left, and it is unbearable."

Parents in our sample did express a few hopes. The one that came up most frequently—twenty times—was the hope that research would find a cure. Other hopes frequently expressed for their children were for better housing, a more normal life, society's acceptance, more self-sufficiency, freedom from relapses and a few friends.

Many parental responses seemed ambivalent: a mixture of hanging on and giving up hope. Bennett and Bennett (1984, p. 560) capture this phenomenon well:

> Nevertheless, the abandonment of false hope permitted a redefinition of the sense of self-esteem based on an acceptance of the limits of probable change and of the responsibility for change. In these cases, clinical improvement and a more realistic ability to plan for the future resulted from the abandonment of hope.

Terkelson (1987, p. 160) writes about "The Collapse of Optimism":

> Often the hope that the illness would pass has enabled the family to cope. To the extent that hope of cure has played a part in the family's coping repertoire, the chronicity of SMI constitutes an assault on their ability to support the patient's hope. The picture is complicated: cure is out of reach, but some form of aliveness and coping is attainable. Yet valuing the latter is difficult so long as hope of cure is retained.
>
> Eventually the collapse of hope sets in motion another process: mourning the loss of the loved one; the image of another person held in the minds of family members.

Could it be that part of the coping repertoire for parents involved giving up some measure of hope? And that, in contrast, clients have to hang on to hope to survive?

The parents we interviewed seemed to be "supercopers" (a term coined by Hatfield and Lefley, 1987). It both touches and impresses me to see how many people can lead reasonably happy lives with despair and hopefulness residing side by side. Perhaps we underestimate this aspect of the human condition: the capacity to build a good life atop a platform of sadness.

Professionals' Perspectives

We did not find literature by professionals dealing specifically with their hopes for mentally ill clients, but we interviewed fifty health care professionals from Wisconsin and Michigan who worked primarily with clients diagnosed with SMI. The average age of the thirty females and twenty males was 41.5 years. On average, they had been in their professions for 14.3 years.

The nature of hope differs for professionals and families. The most obvious difference has to do with bonding. Professionals may care deeply about a client, but their hopes, dreams, and grief cannot be compared to those of the family. The direct pain expressed by professionals was not as intense as for clients and parents, for instance. After all, the parent–child bond is usually the strongest bond there is.

Another difference has to do with how hopes arise. Professionals tend to enter the picture during the deterioration or crisis of a client. This means they often see the person at his or her worst. Their hopes for the client thus start from much lower baselines than those of families, who start with high hopes for the person's future and then have to lower those hopes drastically after the illness develops.

Professionals, clients, and families may start with different hopes, but the beliefs and attitudes of one group often influence the others. Unfortunately, it is often the case that professionals' grim outlooks about SMI dim the hopes of the others or lead to a vicious cycle of low expectations and low hopes. As Harding and colleagues (1987) pointed out, professionals do not see those clients who are doing so well that they no longer seek out professional services. Thus, expectations of deterioration and deficit states "have pervaded and guided clinical judgments, treatment programming policy formulation, and priority funding decisions and have stripped hopes of recovery from many patients and their families."

Meanwhile, in our interviews, professionals did express hopes and concerns regarding their SMI clients. A social worker who had been in the field for twenty-five years said: "I hope for my clients to suffer less." A worker who had just started in the field said: "I hope they can find peace and harmony within themselves."

The hope most often mentioned (37 percent of respondents) was that clients would accept their illnesses. "I hope she can learn to accept her illness, and I do wish these folks could be accepted without stigma."

Next often (35 percent) was the hope that clients would manage their medications successfully and control side effects, thus enabling the highest possible level of functioning. The professionals we interviewed also hoped that research would find a cure. One young psychiatrist talked about his hopes for better medications. Then he paused and said, rather wistfully: "If they could have a little sparkle in their eyes . . .."

The data from our fifty interviewees reflected genuine concern and caring for clients, but the searing pain of the clients and the parents was absent. Professionals expressed a lot of hope for better community support programs, more independence for their clients, an improvement in daily living skills, and better housing. In short, these hopes were comparatively task-centered.

The level of knowledge about SMI and medications was high among the people we interviewed. It was also heartening to see that they did not resort to family blaming, and they showed a great deal of compassion for people suffering with SMI.

Clinical Implications

So what are the clinical implications of this? Our data is skewed in the direction of people with SMI who can articulate quite well, either verbally or by writing. We do not hear much from the sicker people or from those who have recovered or gotten so much better that they are no longer involved with social services. But even with what we do have, our exploratory study shows that parents, people with SMI, and professionals often have different hopes. Hopes and expectations of one group can influence another. Hope has a high contagion factor, as does lack of hope.

In terms of keeping hope alive, if we proceed as if what we do is in the best interests of clients and families alike, we may be wrong. To be most helpful, we may need to proceed along quite different lines for parents and clients, for instance. It is possible to work in two different directions at the same time if we know what is needed and what we are doing with respect to people's hopes.

Most of our interviewees with SMI expressed little hope. Considering how devastating these illnesses are and how miserably our society treats mentally ill people, this finding is not surprising. The sadness of this is in the pain of living without hope.

Scotland (1969, p. 158) theorizes about the importance of hope for people with schizophrenia:

> The present theory would also predict that the hopelessness of the schizophrenic person would destroy any motivations to achieve goals in the real world. With little hope, there is little basis for actively dealing with the world. In turn, the failure consequent upon the lack of coping only confirms the hopelessness, in turn leading to even more withdrawal. The vicious circle has begun.

Our 1989 study is descriptive and exploratory, and the only family members we interviewed about hope were parents and SMI adults. We do not have information about the hopes of other family members. It is conceivable that siblings, spouses, children, and extended family differ in this area. This chapter is intended to stimulate consideration about differing perspectives on hope. To be without hope is to give up, and yet many of the clients we spoke to were gentle, good humored, and appreciative of our study. Perhaps some were hanging on to a shred of hope. We are not sure. We do know they are courageous people.

References

Backlar, P. (1994). *The family face of schizophrenia.* New York: J. P. Tarcher/Putnam Books.

Bennett, M. I., & Bennett, M. B. (1984, Apr.). The uses of hopelessness. *American Journal of Psychology, 141*(4), 559–560.

Brown, R. (1993). *The second son of God.* Australia: Ray Brown (P. O. Box 654, Glebe, NSW, Australia 2037).

Deveson, A. (1991). *Tell me I'm here.* Australia: Penguin Books.

Folkard, L. (1992). *The rock pillow*. Australia: Fremantle Arts Centre Press (193 S. Terrace, S. Fremantle, W. Australia 6162).

Godschalx, S. M. (1987). Experiences and coping strategies of people with schizophrenia. Doctoral dissertation. University of Utah College of Nursing.

Gregory, S. (1952). *In search of sanity: Journal of a schizophrenic*. New Hyde Park, NY: University Books.

Harding, C. M., Zubin, J., Strauss, J. S. (1987, May). Chronicity in schizophrenia: Fact, partial fact, or artifact? *Journal of Hospital and Community Psychiatry, 38*(5), 477–486.

King, L. P. (1964). Criminal complaints: A true account. In B. Kaplan (Ed.), *The inner world of mental illness*. New York: Harper & Row.

Lefley, H., & Hatfield, A. (Eds.) (1987). *Families of the mentally ill: Coping and adaptation*. New York: Guilford.

The Lighthouse (1987). A consumer's newsletter (no longer extant). Madison, WI.

Moorman, M. (1992). *My sister's keeper: Learning to cope with a sibling's mental illness*. New York: Norton.

North, C. S. (1987). *Welcome, silence*. New York: Simon & Schuster.

Sinnett, R. E. (1964). The diary of a schizophrenic man. In B. Kaplan (Ed.), *The inner world of mental illness*. New York: Harper & Row.

Spaniol, L., Zipple, A. M., Lockwood, D. (1993). The role of the family in psychiatric rehabilitation. *Innovations and Research, 2*(4), 27–33.

Terkelson, K. G. The meaning of mental illness to the family. In A. Hatfield & H. Lefley (Eds.), *Families of the mentally ill: Coping and adaptation* (pp. 128–142). New York: Guilford. Vonnegut, M. 91975). *The Eden Express*. New York: Praeger.

Wilson, L. (1968). *This stranger, my son*. New York: Putnam Books.

The following chapter is dedicated to my friend and colleague Dr. Mary Ann Test, who taught me by example the enormous importance of listening to and learning from others.

XII

LIVING IN THE TOWER OF BABEL

People with mental illness, family members, educators, reachers, clinicians, religious leaders, and policy makers have multiple perspectives on SMI and what needs to be done in every conceivable situation. Take the issue of etiology, for example. Many parents feel some relief during this "decade of the brain," as researchers are finding that SMI seems to be primarily biological and genetic in origin rather than due to family interaction. Such knowledge relieves parents of their crippling guilt. Many children and siblings of people with SMI do not like this notion, though, because it increases their fears of developing an SMI or passing it on to their children. People with SMI also disagree about etiology. If it is primarily genetic, they may feel relieved of responsibility for their illness, but at the same time hopeless: they cannot be cured.

Here we have an example of differing perspectives within just one group, family members. If we look at other groups, the plot thickens. Educators are supposed to teach the different perspectives about etiology with academic objectivity. But they have strong beliefs and biases depending on the era in which they were educated, their personal experiences, and how well they have kept up on the research. The same holds true for clinicians. Policy makers who believe SMI's origins to be largely environmental look toward policies of prevention. Those who think more in terms of biological causes lean toward programs offering a continuum of care. Religious leaders have taken a lead in providing shelters for homeless people, many of whom are mentally ill. We know very little about their beliefs about the origins of SMI.

Major Issues

Etiology is just one small example of the complex issues surrounding SMI. Endless possibilities for disagreement include questions of treatment, asylum vs. community care, freedom (for whom?), autonomy vs. dependency, legal issues and civil rights, and homelessness. Much is not known about SMI, which is the ideal fermenting ground for differing perspectives, poor listening skills, and a great deal of fighting. People who do not know much about SMI tend to be the most sure of what is right and what is wrong. Those who know the most usually are the least opinionated and can more easily see the pros and cons for various positions.

This chapter ends with suggested ways of working together in a context of conflict. First, though, it discusses some of the different issues and perspectives among broad groups of people, some of the differing views within the same groups, and what each group wishes the other understood about its perspective. The groups are: people with SMI, their families, clinicians, researchers, educators, and policy makers. Many other important groups—religious affiliates, police officers, people in the criminal justice system, and so forth—are involved in the care of SMI people, but we know little of their beliefs about SMI.

The accompanying diagram obviously only scratches the surface. There are circles within circles, and any of us may belong to several simultaneously. Many of us speak and write as if we were speaking on behalf of entire groups. We are not. Each group represents many views and beliefs. Perhaps the miracle is that we are moving forward at all. If we understand or at least respect each other more, we may be in a better position to accept the reality of our legitimate differences, instead of focusing on them and fighting.

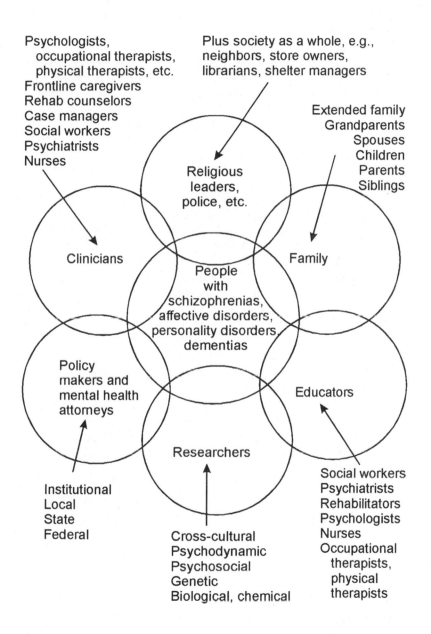

Psychologists,
occupational therapists,
physical therapists, etc.
Frontline caregivers
Rehab counselors
Case managers
Social workers
Psychiatrists
Nurses

Plus society as a whole, e.g.,
neighbors, store owners,
librarians, shelter managers

Extended family
Grandparents
Spouses
Children
Parents
Siblings

Religious
leaders,
police, etc.

Clinicians

Family

People
with
schizophrenias,
affective disorders,
personality disorders,
dementias

Policy
makers and
mental health
attorneys

Educators

Researchers

Institutional
Local
State
Federal

Cross-cultural
Psychodynamic
Psychosocial
Genetic
Biological, chemical

Social workers
Psychiatrists
Rehabilitators
Psychologists
Nurses
Occupational
therapists,
physical
therapists

We all approach SMI with our own values, beliefs, biases, educations, and experiences. It can be hard to stand in the shoes of others long enough to respect and take into consideration their perspectives. If we can do so, however, we become less inclined to run roughshod over one another, more inclined to cooperate and compromise as needed. Deveson's (1992) conversation between a parent and a social worker illustrates two different worlds:

> I found a social worker and then wished I hadn't. She wore sandals and a denim skirt, touched my arm several times, and spoke with a rising inflection at the end of every sentence. I decided she had taken a counseling course by correspondence.
> "Try not to be down-hearted."
> "But what am I going to do?"
> "Show him you love him."
> "But what-am-I-going-to-do?"
> I stared at her. I could feel tears of frustration pricking behind my yes. "It's not like that," I shouted. The social worker hopped in quickly. "Why don't you draw up a contract together and stick it up somewhere handy? Like the door of your fridge." She smiled graciously.
> I am wary of such contracts. They sounded like a good idea in the parenting manuals, but whenever I tried them on my children, they said: "You're weird!"

The challenge of understanding other perspectives is more or less steep depending on the issue under discussion.

A definitive list of issues would stretch into infinity, so just a few are touched on here to illustrate this basic idea.

DEINSTITUTIONALIZATION VS. ASYLUM

One of the most controversial issues since the 1950s has been whether to deinstitutionalize people with SMI or to provide them with asylum and protection. Most thinking people would agree that it is not an either/or issue, and that a broad continuum of care is needed. But given that we do not yet have such a system of care, huge numbers of people with SMI are not being cared for adequately. Many are forced to deal with a harmful either/or situation.

Most SMI people prefer to be out of psychiatric institutions of any kind. Do they prefer jails, homeless shelters, and the streets to mental hospitals? The evidence points in that direction. When we see the deplorable conditions under which many such people live, including homelessness, some of us find this concept hard to grasp.

It had always seemed to me that a humane, well-run hospital would be better than the streets and shelters. Then, for a few weeks, some students and I interviewed older people with SMI in a mental hospital where they had spent all of their adult lives. They were broken shadows of people without hopes of any kind. Speaking with them had an enormous impact on my thinking. (Still, having a system of small, compassionately run, *unlocked* hospitals for those in need of asylum and protection would probably be better than having only the streets and homeless shelters.)

Many family members feel the need for easier admission to hospitals for their SMI relative during psychotic episodes. The ill relative desperately needs care, and family members eventually feel exhausted, overwhelmed, and unable to cope. Obviously, many SMI people and their families have differing perspectives on the subject of deinstitutionalization versus asylum.

Educators, researchers, and clinicians can and do find all sorts of literature to prove why one side or the other of the debate is best. Volumes have been written on the topic. Some people value freedom and civil rights above all else; others are more concerned about food, shelter, and safety. There are no rights or wrongs here, just endless complexities—and a desperate need for a continuum of care to meet the needs of this population.

Policy makers have in mind yet another priority: saving money. Many of them want deinstitutionalization. On the other hand, everyone wants the streets to be safe, and no one wants to confront the guilt, pity, anger, and confusion of seeing homeless and mentally ill people on the streets. Policy makers thus sometimes call for reinstitutionalization. Here again, the complexities are vast. Policy makers try to save money reflect societal values, please everyone, and get reelected or reappointed.

MEDICATIONS AND/OR INVOLUNTARY COMMITMENT

When watching a person who is actively psychotic—hearing voices and seeing things we cannot see—it seems obvious to CNPs (Dr. Fred Frese's wonderful term for "chronically normal person") that medication to stop the symptoms is the only sensible intervention. But CNPs do not know how these medications feel. Family members and clinicians report that some people with SMI say that they do not want to give up their voices. They are desperately lonely, they say, and the voices are their only company.

The side effects are dreadful, say others. So are the side effects of chemotherapy for cancer, argue the parents and professionals; but the alternative is death, so people take them. In mental illnesses, argue the consumers, the alternatives are not death. Life without meds is worse than death, say some family members. On and on the debate rages. No simple answers, though I have always liked the solution suggested by Howell, Diamond, and Wikler (1981): they recommended a three-week trial of medications with the patient's permission for such having been given to the psychiatrist during a nonpsychotic state. Three weeks is usually enough time for medications to take effect, at which time SMI people are in a better position to make decisions about what they then want to do.

Consumer opinions vary: some SMI people see medication as the deliverance from damnation; some, as the ultimate in horror. Others hold every opinion in between. A lot depends on the person's degree of disability, past experiences with the mental health system and with medications, and feelings about authority, age, and so on.

Researchers in the biomedical field are looking for better medications, researchers in the psychosocial field are looking at environmental factors that influence SMI. Their feelings about medications vary, depending on their education, values, biases, and experiences. The same holds true for clinicians.

Medications and involuntary commitment are really two separate issues and ought not be lumped together. This chapter does so for two reasons. One, both issues involve civil rights. Two, a rather inconsistent and strange situation exists at the present time. If people with SMI are found to be a danger to themselves, laws allow their involuntary commitment to a hospital. But that does not necessarily mean they can be medicated without their consent. For some of us, that makes about as much sense as admitting someone for a broken leg but then not being able to set the leg. Others argue that protecting people's lives by hospitalization is still not grounds for violating their civil rights with involuntary medications. Maybe.

Educators, policy makers, clinicians, attorneys, family members, and consumers can and do run the whole gamut. Civil libertarians take the position that absolutely no circumstances warrant involuntary commitment or medication. The other extreme maintains that a person in a psychotic state is in no position to make those decisions, and a doctor should be able to decide instead.

No solutions come to mind. Listening carefully to each other and trying to get a feel for what is behind the strong feelings and opinions may enhance our ability to work together and find compromises.

AUTONOMY VS. DEPENDENCE

Our North American culture is ambivalent about autonomy and dependence. In many ways we still have a frontier mentality that admires the independent person who takes charge of his or her life. We are proud to "pull ourselves up by our own bootstraps." At the same time, another theme expresses the anomie, the isolation, and the meaninglessness that so many feel in our culture. Human beings are social animals, and too many people today feel lonely and disconnected from others. Those who struggle with SMI feel this a thousandfold more than others. Additionally, our culture reacts to socially disparate people by taking charge, controlling their lives, and making them dependent.

It is interesting to note that all cross-cultural studies done on the schizophrenias show that these illnesses are less devastating to people in developing countries. Several explanations exist: closer family ties, simpler jobs available, and people's tendency to approve of dependency and interdependency more in those countries.

Our cultural attitude plays itself out in our myriad opinions and actions surrounding autonomy. In the SMI area our jargon is full of slogans about the "least restrictive" treatment or living environment, and "reaching one's full potential." We emphasize employment and psychosocial rehabilitation. Perhaps people with SMI would survive a lot better in an environment that approved of interdependency or at least did not look down on dependency.

But we live in this culture, and most people with SMI want to be independent. They resent their dependency. Family members desire independence for loved ones and simultaneously fear they will not be able to make it on their own. Policy makers talk about gridlock in group homes and other living arrangements that provide treatment. They want SMI people to get better and move on. But moving on often means deterioration for those who need a high level of care and protection. Clinicians are often pressured into making treatment plans they know are not in the best interests of their clients.

An example of this is in discharge planning from mental hospitals. For fiscal reasons, clinicians often have to discharge patients before they are ready. Aside from their clinical treatment not being complete, such patients are frequently released into totally inadequate living situations (e.g., a homeless shelter) because nothing else exists in that community.

There is a solution to this one: to provide a continuum of care and housing that accommodates everything from total dependency to independence. Given that severe mental illnesses affect their sufferers along the full range from autonomy to dependence, this is a more realistic approach.

CONFIDENTIALITY VS. INFORMATION SHARING

Another area fraught with craziness is the client's right to confidentiality. People in treatment should not be stigmatized and gossiped about, and their privacy should be protected. In reality, however, the laws governing confidentiality frequently keep both families and clinicians from receiving the information they need to provide the best care for people. For instance, when a person is floridly psychotic and is lost or in an emergency room, jail, or shelter, it surely would be helpful to be able to call a mental health center and find out who his or her doctor is, what medications have been prescribed, and if there is a significant friend or relative who should be notified. This is not feasible under current laws.

In our interviews with spouses, we were particularly struck by how often they felt lost and put down by how professionals handled confidentiality. Their ill partners were giving inaccurate, harmful information when psychotic; and spouses had no chance to voice their own accounts. Then, when the ill spouses came back home, professionals gave the well partners no idea of what was going on or how to best provide care. Under the guise of confidentiality, attending clinicians told them very little.

People in these professions have also expressed frustration about needing information about clients and either having to jump through many hoops to get it or not be able to get it at all. Researchers can be delayed or even stopped in their work by review committees that at times are overly fussy on the subject of confidentiality. We definitely need ethics and laws on confidentiality, as many abuses have occurred in the past. We also need more adequate solutions so that people who are in a position to be helpful can get the information they need.

Differing Perspectives Within Groups

In addition to existing among groups, different perspectives abound within the same groups. Not all families agree on issues, nor all consumers, researchers, clinicians, policy makers, or educators. In families, for example, opinions vary among parents, siblings, spouses, children of SMI parents, grandparents, and other extended family members. Age and stage of development are going to influence any family member.

As mentioned earlier, we interviewed two siblings from the same family. One had grown up during her mentally ill mother's period of positive (florid and even violent) manifestations of her illness. The other had grown up when her mother's symptoms were largely negative; the mother had spent most of her time quietly in the bedroom. These two siblings had very different ideas about the illness and about what should have been done. Neither could understand the other's perspectives on their mother.

Parents usually carry the biggest burden, as they find it hard to walk out of the situation. Siblings, however, do have options: "I'm out of here" was an oft-heard response in our study. Extended family members often do not have a clear picture of what is going on and may have strong opinions. Closer or more involved relatives may resent their perspectives, feeling that more distant relatives do not really understand the situation. The family member who is totally wedded to a biomedical explanation of the illness gets angry with the family member who believes that psychosocial factors also play a larger role. And when they start to argue, their minds may snap shut more tightly than two steel drums.

Educators and researchers sometimes miss parts of reality if they cloister themselves within the Ivory Tower. (My "professional hat" is trembling. I know many fine researchers and educators who do get out of the tower, and they have as much compassion and concern as any family member.) Some are not as in touch as they should be with what is going on in the trenches. Like everyone else, they have differing interests, beliefs, and areas of expertise. Those who are looking at viruses as an explanation for some forms of SMI will want money, time, and energy for their research. Those who are convinced that high levels of expressed emotion have a profound effect on people with SMI want to do research in that direction, and so on. Mental illnesses abound, are distinct, and are very complex in both etiology and treatment. We need all the research and help we can get.

Different disciplines emphasize different aspects of concern, as well they should. Psychiatrists are very involved in medications. Social workers are more concerned with case management, meeting basic needs, and planning treatment. Depending on where they work, professionals are concerned about good institutional or community care, or both.

Not only do people have different disciplines, training and areas of expertise, but the era in which they were trained also influences their thinking. Someone trained in the 1950s who has not kept abreast of later findings is apt to emphasize psychodynamic theories of causality and treatment. A more recent graduate will have been heavily influenced by the biomedical model.

Clinicians are also influenced by their job circumstances. How good are their working conditions, pay, and status? What is their usual caseload? Do they enjoy the respect of their supervisors and directors? Do they have a working relationship with the local AMI group? What is the political climate of their community? All these variables and more influence their work.

Policy makers often get caught between a rock and a hard place. Everyone is trying to influence them. They do not necessarily have special training about SMI, and their job is to pay more attention to fiscal matters and politics than other aspects of a problem. There is no reason to hold contempt for such concerns; even the best policy makers cannot accomplish anything if they do not get money and are not reelected or reappointed.

Consumers suffer the most, have very strong opinions, and disagree (as well as agree) among themselves. First of all, their illnesses—the affective disorders, schizophrenias, personality disorders, and dementias—are all different and have various levels of severity. It is therefore troublesome when one individual or group tries to speak for all. Family members and consumers tend to speak from their own experience. How could it be otherwise? But the articulate activist who has recovered from schizophrenia cannot speak for the poor catatonic soul who lives locked in the numbness and terror of his or her mind. We can no more compare the two than we can compare superficial skin cancer with advanced melanoma, even though they are both cancers.

Additionally, people with SMI have had very different experiences within their families and at the hands of the mental health and legal systems. This has a tremendous bearing on how they view things. Some people are consumed (understandably) by their anger. They have had terrible experiences in hospitals, in jails, with medications, and with prejudices of our society. Others feel gratitude for some helpful and kindly treatment they received. Age, cultural background, degree of helplessness or hopefulness, family involvement, and many other variables play big roles in how consumers feel about the many issues surrounding care, treatment, and who should be running the show. If this chapter has one overriding theme, it is that no individual has the right to speak for all others; nor can one group speak for all other groups.

I have discussed a few of the main areas of conflict, and I want to mention the areas in which considerable agreement exists among and within groups. Most of us agree that decent housing is a must, along with adequate food and clothing. Most people agree that research is important and desperately hope for improved treatment, to say nothing of hoping for cures and prevention. It is probably safe to say that most groups see the benefits of social programs and rehabilitation. Most peole also agree about the devastating effects of loneliness and wish for ways to alleviate this anguish.

"What I Want You To Know About My Perspective"

The ideas in this section are based on many informal conversations as well as formal workshops over a fifteen-year period. Across the country, I have done workshops with AMI and NAMI groups, mental health centers, and different agencies working with people with SMI. Conversing with consumers and with policy makers, living and working among educators and researchers, and training students to work in this area have also influenced my thinking. In the last year I have sent letters to people in all these categories, telling them about this chapter and asking for their opinions about what it is they wish others to know about their perspectives.

Again, most of this information is volunteered and it is by no means a cross sample or a random sample. So I make no claims to having the definitive opinions. These are just some deeply felt things that many people were eager to share, and for which I am grateful.

CONSUMERS

Research on consumer perspectives all points in the same direction. People with SMI suffer enormously, they grieve for their lost lives, they wish to pass for "normal," they worry about economic and emotional protection, they feel the terrible stigma and prejudices of our society toward them and, like all people everywhere, they yearn for friendship, respect, love, happiness, and some meaning to their lives.

When I asked what they want family members and mental health workers to know about them, consumers' most common message was the desire for much more say in their treatment and care. My impression is that many people with SMI are acutely aware of the pain and stress their illness has created within the family, and they feel very sad about this. Other themes among our respondents were: conflicts between dependency and autonomy; wanting to work but being afraid of failure; and the agony of accepting a chronic illness.

In many ways, taking medications forces a consumer to face the issue of chronicity, which partially explains the resistance to medications. The medications also feel terrible. Sue Estroff's

(1981) chapter on medications in her book *Making It Crazy* is one of the best descriptions of this double bind consumers feel around the issue of medications. I highly recommend the chapter.

FAMILIES

The last fifteen years have seen more and more litera-ture from parents, and I think most of it is excellent. (The National Alliance for the Mentally Ill has up-to-date reference lists on this literature.) Parents wish that everyone in our culture understood that mental illnesses are diseases as real as cancer or diabetes; that people with these illnesses suffer the tortures of the damned; and that people with SMI deserve as much sympathy and attention as people with other illnesses get. Our hearts ache for our loved ones because of the stigma and misunderstandings they encounter constantly. It is terrible to have to suffer with these illnesses. To compound that with society's hostility and prejudice is an unten-able misery.

Parents ask of the outside world, "Please understand the chronicity and magnitude of our loss and grief." To professionals, they say: "Educate and inform us. Consult appropriately with us, as we are the experts on our child. And make us part of the treatment plans." To the policy makers and researchers, parents plea for more money directed toward community care and toward better medi-cations. Our greatest hopes, of course, are for eventual cures or, better yet, prevention of SMI.

One observation I have made over the years, but not seen anyone write about, is that some parents feel a certain sadness and confusion when they see consumer advocates who are func-tioning very well. For years, these parents compared their suffering loved ones to "normal" people. Now, once again, they feel inferior to advocates who have SMI but are doing much better, compara-tively. "Why can't my Jim do this? Maybe if I could get him to join the consumer movement? What are we doing wrong?" It is sad. Envy-ing a consumer who is doing better than our own relatives also produces guilt.

Shame is another difficult emotion parents feel. To feel ashamed of our adult children because they look strange, smell bad, or act oddly is a terrible feeling.

Siblings, children, spouses, grandparents, and other extended family members also responded to the question: "What do you want others to know about your perspectives?" Siblings wanted their voices to be heard. They especially did not want to be ignored by professionals. And they wanted their families to recognize that they too had problems and concerns. As with their parents, siblings wished that the outside world better understood the havoc that SMI wreaks upon families.

Children who grew up with mentally ill parents felt very strongly about professionals ignoring their helplessness and fear. The younger they were during the course of their respective parents' illness, the more they questioned our present policy of trying to keep families together at all costs. Children want professionals to know of their existence, and then to make a concerted effort to help them survive the chaos and neglect in the household. They also are very concerned about stigma and prejudice directed against mentally ill people.

Spouses wanted professionals and families to hear their side of the story. They particularly want to convey that what professionals see as withholding information because of confidentiality, spouses perceive as being ignored. "They use 'confidentiality' as an excuse not to bother with us," said most spouses. Those we interviewed also expressed a wish that the outside world recognized their social isolation and included them more.

Grandparents expressed more concern for their children and grandchildren than for themselves. As did all the relatives we interviewed, they felt strongly the effects of society's prejudices toward mentally ill people.

Extended family members often felt excluded by the nuclear families. They did not express any particular messages for professionals. But they did say of their families: "Tell us what is going on." They wanted their SMI relative's family to know they were willing to help out but needed direction as to how to do so.

Once again I feel the need to qualify these messages. Our sample was small, and they were all volunteers. We cannot generalize these findings to represent all relatives in all parts of the country. Nor do we know anything about relatives who do not wish to be involved.

POLICY MAKERS

According to the responses I got, many of the people in power would like us to understand the enormous complexities involved in forming policies in a system that devotes very little money and few other resources to the plight of SMI people. We live in a world that gives more money to the military than it does to keeping people alive; a world that spends more money to land one person on the moon than to feed millions of homeless people. Policy makers are looking for the greatest good for the most people at the least possible cost—financially, politically, and otherwise.

Policy makers are also in the tough position of facing pressure from many constituents, all with different agendas. Perhaps we need to spend more time educating, helping, and understanding policy makers and a little less time fighting them. If they do not respond favorably to problems and issues surrounding SMI, then we can try to vote them out and elect more competent people.

Themes from administrators and policy makers included: wanting to remain in direct contact with people and their families; wanting people to call them about problems; needing to stay focused on the big picture and not just the individual; and wanting others to know that policy makers *do* have visions and dreams of how to make things better—if only they had adequate funding.

EDUCATORS

Next to family members, educators in the university system are the people I know best. I am biased by virture of being surrounded by some of the best in the country. So take what I write with a grain of salt.

What do educators in the SMI field want you to know about them? They care very deeply and are doing their best. For the most part, they chose this field because they care deeply. Some of them have mentally ill relatives, some do not. Many educators without SMI family members shed tears over the plight of the mentally ill, just like those who have SMI in the family.

Training people to work with SMI populations has not been a popular field, but it is gaining ground. NAMI's "Curriculum and Training" component has been making monumental and successful efforts at updating the curriculum in professional schools of social work, psychiatry, nursing, psychology, and vocational rehabilitation. (I suspect that educators in schools of medicine, occupational and physical therapy, and other disciplines have been doing the same.) This means including the latest research findings in both the social and biological sciences.

Today's educators also generally convey a more humble attitude about what is and is not known. They are acknowledging the need to listen to people with SMI as well as the need to listen to families. It is heartening to see their ever-increasing use of consumers and family members to bring their personal perspectives into the classroom.

RESEARCHERS

I did not send letters to researchers asking for their perspectives. This section is based on my own impressions, from reading reports and attending countless meetings where researchers presented their findings. In short, much of the foregoing section about educators also applies to people doing research about SMI.

Nonresearchers may underestimate the complexities of the brain and human behavior, and the limitations of the scientific method. While we are living in the "decade of the brain" and have learned more about its working in the past fifteen years than in the hundreds that went before, in some ways we are still in the dark about SMI. It is probably going to be a long, hard struggle before we have cures, let alone preventive approaches.

Part of the struggle is financial. The federal government has cut research funds, governors and regents have cut university budgets, and money is in short supply for training professionals and carrying out good studies. These are very real problems
for researchers, in   both the "hard" sciences and the social
sciences.

As I think about some of the top researchers in the field
of SMI, two vivid scenes come to mind. One was at a NAMI convention where six bright young researchers got awards for their
work and spoke about how much they needed the enthusiasm and
emotional support of family members. They see our suffering, and
they want to help.

Another such memory is from a 1986 NAMI/NIMH meeting in Wasington, DC. A well-known researcher, Dr. Sam Keith,
closed his paper on the state of the art in research on SMI with the
following quote from Horatio. Horatio's commander had sent a
messenger to ask, "How goes the battle, Horatio?"

"Tell him," Horatio responded, "the battle goes well, it is
the troops who truly suffer."

Sam Keith brought tears to my eyes then, and again
now as I write this. For the quality of such researchers, we can all be
grateful.

CLINICIANS

Clinicians are the professionals who are in the trenches
doing some of the front-line work. For years, parents having been
saying: "Hear us! This is how we feel . . . and this is how you make us
feel when you do not listen." In preparation for this chapter, many
clinicians took the time to say, "Hear us. This is how we feel . . .."

Family members, particularly parents, are still in a back-
lash mode from the terrible family-blaming days. In our pain, we
may not have had the energy to think about how some of the front-
line workers feel, or how we might support them occasionally so
that they can hang in there with our loved ones all the longer. As
one social worker said to me years ago at a workshop: "Did it ever

occur to you that we too cry about our clients?" No, it had not occurred to me until that day.

We asked forty-five clinicians what they wanted families and others to know about their work experiences in the SMI field. Thirty-five responses were from social workers, five from nurses, and five from psychiatrists. These clinicians all work in a city that has a national reputation for having state-of-the-art programs for people with SMI. I therefore do not know whether these responses are typical of others throughout the country.

Clinicians described three different areas of concern: their job frustrations, their feelings toward clients, and how families could help them in their work.

JOB FRUSTRATIONS

The lack of funding on all levels—local, state, and federal—underlies all the major frustrations reported by clinicians. "To provide less than optimal services is frustrating and demoralizing for all of us." Many workers discussed the poor funding for both SMI people and for themselves, as exemplified by their low salaries. This is a reflection, they feel, of the low status society attributes to SMI people and the professionals who chose to work with them. We heard:

> I loved my job. I experienced low self-esteem when I got paid, and when I functioned as a cab driver in getting people to their psychiatrists. I worked with some people for the whole four years, drove them to their psychiatrists, and in some cases, never met the psychiatrists. The huge gap between my salary and those in the medical profession infuriated me.

and

> At this point, I have also experienced things
> that family members experience: rage at a
> decompensated client in whom I had in-
> vested a lot of time, frustration that the actions
> of one of my clients would render my hopes
> for him or her irrelevant, and anger at the
> community because it refused to invest in
> housing for our mentally ill.

Too few resources, low pay, and heavy caseloads lead to frequent
turnover among clinicians, which of course has negative effects on
clients and families. In addition, some people complained that their
organizations had inadequate staff in precisely the positions that
most influence workers' morale and sense of competency. "It is
disheartening and disempowering, for those of us responsible for
promoting empowerment in others, to have supervisors in management positions with neither aptitude nor knowledge in the area."

Such remarks probably come as no surprise to anyone.
Let it serve as a reminder that clinicians often work under very
trying conditions, and they too can become badly demoralized.
They do very difficult work in a culture that gives them comparatively little status, low salaries, and often very difficult work
environments.

In contrast was the enthusiasm we heard from the director of a clubhouse. Clubhouses are a form of day treatment or
recreation for mentally ill people, run by members who have mental
illnesses and by professionals. They make every effort to achieve
equality of power and leadership between consumers and non-
consumers. This particular director told us:

> I hope always to work in the clubhouse
> movement and to convince the best of our
> social work students to do the same. I believe
> that here in the clubhouse we pay very close
> attention to the needs and dreams of our
> members. I think that this place—no closed
> doors, no case records, no psychobabble—is

in some way the best of social work: a con-
fluence of several streams: political activism,
clinical practice and group work.

Workers share with families the frustrations of inadequate housing and programs for SMI people, of mental health laws
that sometimes stand in the way of obtaining treatment and care,
and of stigma against SMI people and the professionals who work
with them. "Very few people have respect for the work we do."

FEELINGS TOWARD CLIENTS

None of our forty-five respondents complained about
clients. There was no "blaming the victim." On the contrary: clients
were usually mentioned under the topic of job satisfaction, as in:

When things improve for a client, or go right
in some way however small I feel intense
joy.

and

Much of the joy of my job as well as the stress
comes from observing and having involvement with the families of my clients. For the
most part, the stress is not from anger or
conflict with families, but from empathizing
with them.

Clinicians spoke of their clients' courage, bravery, and sense of
humor. Many marveled at how these people could go on with their
lives under such adverse conditions. It was heartening to hear these
comments as the rule rather than the exception.
A hospital-based psychiatrist said that "most family
members seem to have dropped away, and I feel very sad about
that." (Could it be that by the time patients need hospitalization, the

family is so exhausted and discouraged that they take this opportunity to get respite care? Perhaps they get reinvolved after the
discharge.) He went on to say about parents:

> If I have hurt you or don't understand, let me
> know. And let me know how I can help. Don't
> let professionals guilt-trip you into doing
> more than you can do. You must let us know
> your limits. But you have to know our limits,
> too. We have no cures, and the negative
> symptoms are so persistent and hard to deal
> with.

From a social worker in a shelter for the homeless
mentally ill:

> When I've seen a client who was at his lowest
> point get into a treatment facility, get stable
> on meds, and come back to the shelter not
> necessarily to say thank you, but just to show
> me how far he's come, I feel so happy.

HOW FAMILIES CAN HELP

Many respondents said that families do not under-
stand the magnitude of the problems clinicians face (just as parents
said clinicians do not understand the magnitude of their pain and
frustrations).

> Look, I have a huge caseload, and just today
> have been assigned a new case of a seventy-
> eight-year-old man with SMI who is homeless
> and sleeping on a park bench. He has no
> family, and he has cancer. Families need to
> know that no one social worker or agency
> can do it all.

On the same topic, another worker who deals primarily with homeless people who have serious mental illness said:

> I guess as a student I never really understood the ramifications of burnout, but as a clinician I deal with it every day. A person has to learn how to relax, how to walk away at 5 p.m., and how to move on when you've exhausted all resources . . . to realize that you cannot change the world or help every client, but you are making a difference.

From a clinician working in a large state hospital:

> The issues of too few resources and (many) legal barriers are often the most frustrating. The system is stretched to its limits, and workers must be creative and relentless in advocating for clients. I face the long wait for services with my clients and their families every day. I realize it is hard for a family to repeatedly hear that I have hit another barrier or it will be another few weeks or months until their relative gets a needed service. As a clinician I am grouped with the system that is maintaining these barriers, yet in order to fight them effectively, I emotionally place myself in alignment with the client. This is a burdensome double bind to be in.

Clinicians also struggle with the mental health system. As one psychiatrist said:

> The hardest part of my job is using and dealing with the crisis intervention team. They make promises they cannot keep, and they take control and power that is beyond their expertise.

A psychiatric nurse in a mental hospital said she wished for honest communication with families. "Tell us your stories. We need to build bridges and avoid polemics." A young social worker said she wanted families to know that "most of us want very much to support them and understand their perspectives. I would like families to know that most of us view them with respect and truly want to alleviate their fear and stress in some way."

As in our interviews with family members, all of our clinicians were also volunteer respondents. Thus, we have a positively biased sample of workers who are proud of their work and eager to be heard. Plenty of horror stories still exist. Most of us have both heard and experienced the negative stories. It is time to acknowledge some of the positives.

I have used this section to report more about clinicians than any other group. This is not meant to imply lesser importance to anyone else. Quite the contrary: we are *all* needed. Rather, this section's length reflects a combination of factors: relatively speaking, many more clinicians responded to my inquiry; it is one perspective I know well (along with those of families); and clinicians are often in the best position to coordinate the planning of treatment. They are the case managers.

POSTSCRIPT

It takes only minutes to make a phone call or write a note that says, "Thank you" or "Well done!" or "I am grateful for your help." Our respondents said that people rarely do this. When it does happen, it makes both sides feel very good and helps promote better relationships all around. Try it!

Summary

Noah's descendants never actually built the Tower of Babel. God prevented them through a confusion of tongues. Likewise, as Lefley (1992) said about the extended field of SMI: "We are now many movements with multiple agendas." This is apparent in our beliefs desires, actions, and even our language. Sharp contrasts in meaning exist between "SMIs" and "people with schizophrenia," for instance: or between "victims" and "consumers." And the contrasts are equally sharp between advocates of asylum and those advocating deinstitutionalization; between those who want to limit "confidential" information to the consumer, and those who want to expand it to include that person's family or caretakers; and so forth.

Some people focus on treatment, some on social change, or education, advocacy, networking research, or housing. Most NAMI members approve of consumer-operated services but want them as "auxiliary rather than alternative to the professionally run system" (Lefley, 1992). This attitude feels like a put-down to some consumers, who feel that consumers should be in primary charge of the mental health system.

Some of us are fired by pain, others by rage, political convictions, intellectual curiosity, religious belief, status, or a combination of these things. Some are no longer fired up but rather burned out. As with the Tower of Babel, we are not going to reach heaven; but it would be nice if we could get out of hell.

To do this, it would help to understand each other's different perspectives, to stand in the shoes of the others, and maybe to throw in a few more "thank you's" for good measure. Out of diversity come the possibilities for creative compromise and solutions.

References

Deveson, A. (1991). *Tell me I'm here*. Australia: Penguin Books.

Estroff, S. (1981). *Making it crazy*. Berkeley: University of California Press.

Howell, T., Diamond, R. J., & Wikler, D. (1981). Is there a case for voluntary commitment? In Beauchamp, Walters, & Leary, *Contemporary issues in bioethics,* 2nd ed. (pp. 163–167). Belmont, CA: Wadsworth.

Keith, S. J., & Lowery, H. A. (1990). How goes the battle? In H. P. Lefley & D. L. Johnson, *Families as allies in treatment of the mentally ill* (pp. 163–169). Washington, DC: APA Press.

Lefley, H. P. (1992, Oct.). Understanding and celebrating diversity in mental health service systems. Talk presented at a meeting of the CSP Service Improvement Grantees, Bethesda, MD.

XIII

ONE VOICE

> Part of the trauma of mental ill-
> ness in a family is the bewildering
> feeling of being alone—all, all
> alone . . .
>   —Monty Berger, president of
>   AMI-Quebec, 6/3/92

This book is descriptive and impressionistic in nature. It is limited in its research techniques and does not incorporate the type of controls that would permit drawing conclusions, beyond the obvious one: severe mental illness is like a skipping stone that has enormous ripple effects on the entire family.

Reading about what various relatives and professionals who have told us about their experiences may stimulate a lot of thinking. In the process, perhaps we can become more under-standing and tolerant, of both ourselves and others. Too often in the past, all of us have been quick to jump to explanations, inter-pretations, conclusions, and reactions. Out of lack of knowledge comes insecurity; and out of insecurity, rigidity. We need to slow down and do a better job of listening to what people are telling us about themselves, their experiences, and their beliefs. We need to hear the whole story, or at least as much of it as they can tell us.

Contradictory impressions abound on almost every subject under the sun in the area of SMI and its impact on the family. On the other hand, only a limited amount of information comes into print directly from family members, other than from parents. As we hear more from other relatives, the complexities increase. There is a lot of agony, and no one to blame. Our entire culture is prejudiced against mentally ill people, and much is lacking in our system of care. The ultimate enemy, however, is the illness, and it affects each family member in different ways.

Part of the human condition includes horrible illnesses without cures, be they cancer, AIDS, heart trouble .... You can only get so dead. With both AIDS and mental illneses, we tend to lack compassion and shun the victims. It will be a good day when severe mental illnesses (and AIDS, of course) can evoke the same understanding and compasson from people that other illnesses do. As W. A. Anthony (1992) so eloquently put it: "I believe that much of the chronicity in severe mental illness is due to the way the mental health system and society treat mental illness and not the nature of the illness itself."

If we shunned cancer patients the way our society shuns mental patients, they too would seem odd and act dreadfully. Can you imagine taking an advanced cancer patient to the hospital in a police car, in handcuffs? Or putting people in four-point restraints to treat their symptoms? (In 1993 in my progressive city, the justification for four-point restraints in one hospital was that all else— medication, behavioral programs, and rehabilitation—had failed.) People with severe mental illness are physically restrained when they are violent. At that point, maybe they are violent in large part because they have been treated like animals. Even the old-fashioned padded cell may be better than four-point restraints.

People with severe mental illnesses need to be treated compassionately, and so do their families—each member. We are still in the dark ages when it comes to understanding SMI, but whatever we do know needs to be shared with all concerned. Our past is replete with the horror of what was done to people with epilepsy, or mental retardation, before we understoood these conditions better. Now we do reasonably well with people who have these disabilities. We owe people who have SMI no less.

Now What?

The obvious needs are to fight prejudice and stigma, to educate society about severe mental illness, to invest more money to care adequately for people who have severe mental illnesses, and to invest more time and money into research. We also need to pay more attention to SMI's ripple effects on the entire family. Relatives need to be included, educated, and emotionally supported. McFarlane's (1993) research on multiple-family psychoeducation clearly showed that both the patient and the family benefitted by educational sessions when the entire family was included.

What is needed may be obvious. How to go about achieving it, is something else again. The first thought that comes to mind is the desperate need for education. First and foremost, the people who live with these dreadful illnesses need to be educated about their conditions. If they do not understand why they are having trouble with school, jobs, relationships, voices, and their whole world, what possible explanations can they have for themselves? That the world is against them? (In many ways they are right about that one.) That they are bad and inadequate? All too often that is the conclusion that people with mental illnesses come to; but this is a faulty deduction. In fact, the many people stricken with these damn illnesses who bravely manage to struggle on with their lives probably deserve a medal of valor.

As soon as a diagnosis is made, professionals and family alike should be in the business of helping people with SMI understand their conditions, treatments, and how they and others might be able to help alleviate or manage symptoms. (This can be more difficult for family members, especially at first, because they are so close to it and sometimes overwhelmed with pain.)

Coping with anxiety, voices, and loneliness, and finding meaning in their lives are all issues that need to be addressed. Obviously, this kind of comprehensive education cannot take place in a few hours. It needs to start with the diagnosis and should probably continue forever. I remember the shock I felt when reading Elizabeth Kytle's (1987) compassionate book, *The Voices of Robby Wilde*. Robby, a man with schizophrenia, first started hearing voices at the age of eight. He was middle-aged before anyone helped him to understand that other people could not hear his voices.

People tend to blame themselves for all illnesses, from the common cold ("I shouldn't have gone out without a jacket") to cancer ("I shouldn't have eaten so much fat"). It is no different with severe mental illnesses. Educating people about what is and is not known about their particular illness can reduce self-blame and increase coping capacities. While we are often helpless in controlling the illnesses, we can get better at the endless process of coping.

Many educators still need to update themselves so they can better train the next generation of professionals. Though conditions have improved over recent years, in many ways because of NAMI's work, we still have a long way to go. Too many educators have not kept up with recent research.

In addition to keeping abreast of current findings, educators do well to invite consumers and family members into their classes to help train professionals. In the words of Janet Pederson, after she interviewed family members in August 1992: "Dysfunctional family, multiproblem family—how often I heard these phrases as a professional. My God, how could these families be otherwise with what they are up against?"

Thus far, education of professionals has taken place on the college and university level. Grade schools and high schools should also provide information about mental illnesses in their social studies curricula. The earlier we inform people, the better. Preventing prejudice and stigma is much easier than eradicating it.

This entire book has been a plea to better educate all family members. The many local and regional Alliances for the Mentally Ill developed out of this need for education, which professionals were not addressing adequately. We must continue educating ourselves, and we welcome with open arms the many fine professionals who are now joining our ranks and forming their own. The education and support of family members should start on day one, and ideally continue for as long as the family wants, which may very well be forever. In addition, families need and deserve support, close interaction with health care professionals, and respite care. To lessen the risk of serious mental-health problems and exhaustion for caregivers, we all need to pull together.

How do we reach policy makers, police, clergy, and our neighbors? As we well know from presidential campaigns, wars, and Olympic games, the media influences people tremendously. It can be a negative force, but it could also be a powerfully positive force. We need less of thrillers such as *Psycho* and *Silence of the Lambs,* and much more of shows such as *Promises* and books such as *Call Me Anna* (Duke, 1988). Today's mass media could be the best way to bring about increased understanding, knowledge, and compassion among the largest number of people.

I started this section by saying that, first and foremost, the people who live with SMI need to be educated about these illnesses. One could also say that, first and foremost, our researchers need adequate funding. To get more money for research also means we need to educate people: taxpayers, policy makers, and philanthropists will not allocate enough money until they understand the need for research. And so the cycle continues.

The Voice of Viktor Frankl

One voice stands out more than others for me when I think of everything I've heard about different perspectives on hope, on the endless processes of grief and coping, and on the lack of individual control in all of these. That voice comes from Viktor Frankl. In 1946 he wrote a book, *Man's Search for Meaning,* about his survival in a Nazi concentration camp. Surely one should not equate the horrors of concentration camps to those of severe mental illnesses. But the search for meaning may be the same. Frankl's ability to find deep meaning and purpose to live under the worst of all possible conditions inspired me in the midst of the senseless suffering that ripples out from SMI. This book's continuing popularity in diverse cultures over the past five decades indicates that most people do indeed search and struggle to find meaning in their lives. To bear witness to agony and feel powerless to prevent or stop the unbearable pain and loss are the ultimate in human suffering.

Freud felt that human beings' main concerns were to gain pleasure and avoid pain. Frankl added another major dimension that seems applicable to SMI. His book pointed out that suffering is unavoidable, that our greatest task is to find meaning in life, and that this meaning is to be found in three different ways:

- By creating a work or doing a deed
- By experiencing something or someone deeply
- By the attitude we take toward unavoidable suffering

Frankl wrote that suffering is not necessary to find meaning: "I only insist that meaning is possible even in spite of suffering" (1946, p. 136). "The more one forgets himself by giving himself to a cause to serve, or another person to love—the more human he is and the more he actualizes himself" (p.133).

Because there is no way to end this book by making it all better, let me suggest we try and find some meaning to our lives amidst the chaos and suffering. We do not have to find it by joining the mental health movement. We could find it by volunteering to help clean a city park, or teaching an illiterate person how to read, or doing any of a million things. The ripple effects of mental illness will not go away, and we will continue to rail, rage, cry, and mourn. But in between, maybe we can try to find meaning by doing a good deed, experiencing something deeply, and trying to bring some identity and meaning to the suffering.

Epilogue

The voices of people in the book—those who live with severe mental illness, their many relatives, front-line clinicians, educators, researchers, administrators, policy makers, people who work in shelters for the homeless, the wonderful students wo did most of this interviewing, the man in the store who asked my son for a light—all keep ringing in my ears. You have all taught us so much.

Well, it worked. In the process of writing this book, the three hats that used to crowd my head have blended into one. One hat—one voice—begs for mercy and understanding toward all who live and cope with severe mental illness. If we can live with our different perspectives in such a way as to stay focused on the needs of people with SMI, and also pay attention to each family member, we will all benefit in the end.

My anger swirled around for twenty years, first toward professionals, then toward the legal and mental health systems, and sometimes (forgive me) even toward people with mental illnesses. It is now dissipated, and in its place is an enormous sadness. The anger was easier. Conflict is inevitable; how we deal with conflict is not.

References

Anthony, W. A. (1992). Editorial column, *Innovations & research,*
    4, 1.
Duke, P. (1988). *Call me Anna.* New York: Bantam Books.
Frankl, V. (1946). *Man's search for meaning.* New York: Washington
    Square Press.
Kytle, E. (1987). *The voices of Robby Wilde.* Cabin John, MD:
    Seven Locks Press.
McFarlane, W. R. (1994). Families, patients, and clinicians as part-
    ners: Clinical strategies and research outcomes in single-
    and multiple-family psychoeducation. In H. Lefley & M.
    Wasow (Eds.), *Helping families cope with SMI.* Newark,
    NJ: Gordon & Breach.
Promises (1986). Commercial television program produced by
    Hallmark. Videotape available from Wellness Repro-
    ductions, Inc., 23945 Mercantile Road, Beachwood,
    OH 44122-5924.

Consent To Participate

This consent form was read and signed by all the people we interviewed. We made every effort to make sure they understood it and knew they were free to terminate an interview if they so chose. No one did terminate; all our participants seemed eager to talk.

Consent to Participate

This is a project which seeks to better understand the experiences of family members of people with severe mental illnesses. We will be asking you what your subjective experiences have been as a result of having a mentally ill relative. You will be our teachers. Our questions will be open-ended and you will be in charge of what, and how much you wish to tell us. You can refuse to answer any question; you can terminate the interview at any point.

The interviews will be taped and then transcribed. The tapes will be erased as soon as they are transcribed, and the transcriptions discarded after our study is done. No names will be used. Strict confidentiality will be adhered to at all times.

_____   _____

Study Participant   Date

_____

Agency Permission of client for contact

CONTACT PERSON: Mona Wasow, School of Social Work, University of Wisconsin, Madison, WI 53706 • Phone: 263-6335

Interview Guidelines

We used five different interview guidelines, reflecting the differences between siblings, spouses, children, grandparents, and other extended family of someone with severe mental illness. Each set of guidelines was similar in the following questions or instructions:

1. How has the serious mental illness of your relative affected you?
2. How do you see your future in relation to your relative with mental illness?
3. What do you think causes serious mental illness?
4. In all interviews, the interviewer was instructed to put away pencils, papers, and tape recorders at the very end, and then to ask: "Is there anything more you care to tell me about your experiences as a [child, sibling, cousin, etc.] with a mentally ill [parent, sibling, etc.]?"
5. All interviewees were offered a packet of informational materials about mental illnesses and about local community resources. They were also given our names and telephone numbers in case they had a future need to talk.

Guidelines for Interviewing Adult Children of Mentally Ill Parents

A lot has been written about parents of mentally ill children, but considerably less about children of mentally ill parents.

We must learn much more about the impact of mental illness on children, and will be most grateful to you for anything you can teach us.

A. Data on Your Mentally Ill Parent
  1. Age (or the parent's age at time of death)
  2. Educational level
     a. Mother _____
     b. Father _____
  3. Race, ethnicity
  4. Occupation
  5. Diagnosis
  6. How long has she/he been ill?
  7. At what age did he/she become ill?
  8. Number and length of hospitalizations
  9. Living situation of parent now
  10. Who are the primary supports for your parents now?

B. Data on You
  1. Age
  2. Your age when your parent first became ill
  3. Sex
  4. Race, ethnicity
  5. Degree of religiosity
  6. Occupation
  7. Level of education
  8. Children in the family:
     a. Number of children
     b. Your birth order
  9. Amount of contact with ill parent over your lifespan:
     a. Birth–two years
     b. Age 2–5
     c. Age 5–10
     d. Age 10–18
     e. At the present time
  10. When was your last contact, and how extensive was it?

C. Questions about Your Childhood

1. What was life like in your home as a child?
2. What happened in your family when your parent required hospitalization?
3. What is it like to have a parent with mental illness? What was it like as a child to have a parent with mental illness?
4. When did you realize your parent was ill?
5. Did you know your parent before illness? If so, what was he/she like?
6. Who took care of your parent through the years?
7. Did anyone ever talk to you about your parent's illness? If so, who was that?
8. What did you do to survive? How did you cope?
9. Did you have support from other family members? Extended family?
10. What have your feelings been toward your parent through the years? What are your feelings now?
11. What will the future be like for you and your parent?
12. If your parent exhibited "crazy" behaviors, what did you make of it?
13. What do you think your siblings' views toward your parent are?
14. Did anyone ever do anything that was *not* helpful in dealing with your parent's mental illness?
15. Have you had other role models for a mother/father?

D. Questions about You Now

1. Do you have genetic concerns for yourself or other family members?
2. Would you say your parent's illness has influenced your development as a person?
3. What sorts of feelings do you now have toward your parent, e.g., sadness?
4. What do *you* think caused your parent's illness?

Guidelines for Interviewing Siblings

We assume that a mentally ill relative has an impact on most, if not all, relatives in the family. The variability of this impact is probably tremendous—all the way from being a dominating influence to having very little impact; from severe pain and worry to relatively little concern.

We are interested in knowing how _____'s SMI has influenced you.

A. Data on Your Mentally Ill Relative
1. Age
2. Sex
3. Race, ethnicity
4. Diagnosis
5. Educational level
6. How long has he/she been ill?
7. Living situation of relative now
8. Living situation, in terms of your contact with relative over the years

B. Data on You
1. Age
2. Sex
3. Age you were at the onset of your sibling's illness
4. Marital status
5. Occupation
6. Educational level
7. Income
8. Other siblings (and birth order)
    a. Tell me what your sibling was like before he/she became ill. What was your relationship with him/her like? How did you view him/her?
    b. Tell me about the onset of your sibling's illness. When did you first know that your sibling was ill?
    c. Tell me about those experiences: behaviors, hospitalizations, your feelings about them. [Develop time line of the course of sibling's illness.]

d. What is your understanding of your sibling's illness?
   1) Define it.
   2) What caused it?
e. Where did you get this information?
f. Who helped you deal with these changes in your family?
g. How do you think _____'s illness affected other members of your family?
h. What changes occurred in the family as a result of your sibling's illness?
i. How has the mental illness of your sibling affected your life?
j. What roles or responsibilities do other siblings, parents take in your family, in terms of your mentally ill family member?
k. Has your family had help from mental health professionals? Were you included?
l. How have your feelings toward your sibling changed over the years?
m. How have you survived throughout your sibling's illness? How do you cope? Has religion played any role in helping you?
n. Did you have support from people outside of your immediate family?
o. Who have you talked to regarding your sibling's mental illness over the years? What were their responses?
p. How do you see your future in relation to your sibling?
q. Would you say your sibling's illness has influenced your development as a person? Please explain.

Guidelines for Interviewing Spouses

We assume that a mentally ill spouse has had a tremendous impact on you and other members of your family. We are interested in knowing what having a mentally ill spouse has done to you and your life.

A. Data on Your Mentally Ill Spouse
 1. Age
 2. Sex
 3. Race, ethnicity
 4. Educational level
 5. Diagnosis
 6. How long has he/she been ill?
 7. Living situation of spouse now
 8. How long were you [have you been] married?
 9. How long has she/he been ill?
 10. Number and length of hospitalizations

B. Data on You
 1. Age
 2. Sex
 3. Race, ethnicity
 4. Educational level
 5. Occupation
 6. Income
 7. Number and ages of children
 8. Your degree of religiosity
 9. Present living situation in relation to spouse

C. Questions about Your Marriage
 1. Can you briefly describe your marital situation prior to the illness?
 2. What were the effects on you, as the illness developed?
 3. How did you arrive at your current position, in relation to the marriage?
 4. What kind of supports have there been for you?
    a. From family
    b. From friends
    c. From professionals
    d. In your work situation

5. I assume your spouse's mental illnesses causes all kinds of stresses, everything from "soup to sex." Could you tell me what the main problem area have been for you?
6. What are your coping strategies?

D. Questions About You Now
1. Do you have genetic concerns for your children?
2. Has your spouse's illness influenced your development as an adult?
3. What do you think caused your spouse's illness?
4. What sorts of *feelings* do you now have towards your spouse, e.g., sadness, anger, guilt, love, anger, fear?
5. How do you envision your future?

Guidelines for Interviewing Grandparents

A lot has been written about parents of mentally ill adult children, but nothing has been written about grandparents! This strikes me as a big omission—grandparents are often so important to the entire family. We need to know how grandparents are affected when their grandchild becomes mentally ill. Any information you can share with me will help us to learn more, and I will be most grateful.

It is my hope that if we can know more about how mental illness in the family affects *all* family members, we can be more helpful to everyone.

A. Data on Your Mentally Ill Grandchild
1. Age
2. Sex
3. Race, ethnicity
4. Diagnosis
5. Age at which he/she became ill
6. How long has she/he been ill?

7. Educational level
8. Living situation of your grandchild now
9. How much contact did you have with _____?
    a. Birth to 2 years
    b. 2–5 years
    c. 5–10 years
    d. 10–15 years
    e. 15–20 years
    f. 15 years–present

Note to interviewer: Get *kinds* of contact (telephone calls, letters, face-to-face, etc.) and *depth* of contact. That is, how close to the grandchild did they feel over the years?

B. Data on You
1. Date of birth
2. Sex
3. Race, ethnicity
4. Marital status
5. Occupation or past occupation, if retired
6. Income
    a. Under $10,000
    b. $10,000–$20,000
    c. $20,000–$30,000
    d. Over $30,000
7. How do you see your health now?
    a. Poor
    b. Fair
    c. Good
    d. Excellent

C. Questions about You Now
1. What is your understanding of the diagnosis of [schizophrenia, depression, . . .]?
2. What do you think causes [the particular illness]?
3. How do you think [the grandchild]'s illness has affected:
    a. Your son/daughter?
    b. Your other grandchildren?

4. And what I want to know most about: How has [the grandchild]'s illness affected you?
5. Has [the grandchild]'s illness affected your relationship to your own child [the parent of the mentally ill grandchild]?
6. What do you think will happen to your grandchild in the future?
7. Have any professionals (i.e., social workers, doctors, lawyers, etc.) helped him/her or the family?
   a. Did any of them include you?
   b. Do you wish they had?
8. Has *anyone* or thing (family, friends, professionals, the church, or books) helped you understand _____'s illness?
9. What kind of help, if any, would you want?

Guidelines for Interviewing Extended Family

We have assumed that a mentally ill relative has an impact on most, if not all, family members. The variability of this impact is probably enormous: all the way from being a dominating influence to having very little impact (especially if there was little or no direct contact with the ill relative); from severe pain and worry to relatively little concern.

But we really do not know, because we have not asked you! Quite a bit has been studied and written about some parents of mentally ill children, less about siblings, spouses, and children; and nothing about extended family: aunts and uncles, nieces and nephews, cousins, and grandparents.

Any information you could give us about your experiences would be a starting point, and deeply appreciated. My twenty years of experience—with NAMI, teaching in the area of mental illness, doing workshops, etc.—leads me to believe that the impact of mental illness on the entire family may be greater and more complex than is presently known.

In order to be helpful, we need to know so much more. Please be our teachers.

A. Data on Your Mentally Ill Relative
1. Age
2. Sex
3. Race, ethnicity
4. Diagnosis
5. At what age did your relative become ill?
6. How long has he/she been ill?
7. Living situation of relative now

B. Data on You
1. Age
2. Sex
3. Race, ethnicity
4. Occupation
5. Education level
6. Your relationship to relative (e.g., aunt, nephew, cousin)
7. Age you were when _____ first became ill
8. Amount of contact with _____ over your life span:
   a. Birth to 2 years
   b. 2–5 years
   c. 5–10 years
   d. 10–18 years
   e. 18 years–present
9. When was your last contact, and how extensive was it?

C. General Questions
1. Could you describe your relationship to _____ before: [his/her] illness?
2. Your relationship now?
3. What is your understanding of _____'s illness?
   a. What is it? (i.e., give us your definition of schizophrenia or affective disorder)
   b. What do you think caused the illness?
4. Do you have any genetic concerns for yourself or any of your other relatives?
5. How has _____'s illness affected your life?
6. Will _____'s illness in any way affect your future, do you think?
7. How do you see _____'s illness as having affected [his/her] parents, siblings, grandparents?

APPENDIX **C**

Survey Letter

I sent copies of this letter to various clinicians working with SMI people. From among the responses, we selected samples from social workers, psychiatrists, psychiatric nurses, and administrators.

Our section on professionals also includes data from fifty professionals from Michigan, collected in an earlier study on hope.

School of Social Work
University of Wisconsin–Madison
School of Social Work Building
1350 University Avenue
Madison, WI 53706

March 31, 1993

Dear _____:

In a book I'm writing I am doing a chapter where I'm trying to present the clinician's view of working with SMI people, to family members. I think the time has come for families to hear from you. What is it that families should know about the work problems you face? Your main concerns, worries, hopes, experiences? The satisfactions? Frustrations? What you want from families? How families can be helpful? Hurtful? I would so appreciate any thoughts you have on the subject. Any and all information would be most welcome, to keep me on the right track. You will not be directly quoted without first asking your permission.

Thank you very much.

Sincerely,

Mona Wasow
Clinical Professor

Resources for Family Members

At the end of each interview, the student or social worker asked participants if they wanted a list of local resources for family members. People who said yes received this short resource list. We also answered any questions and sometimes made further recommendations of things to read, depending on people's particular interests.

I. The Alliance for the Mentally Ill of Dane County
    (AMI of Dane County)
    1245 E. Washington Avenue, Suite 292, Madison, WI 53703
    Phone: (608) 255-1695
    A. What is AMI of Dane County?
       "An organization of families and friends of people with long-term mental illness—supporting each other, sharing information, and actively advocating for more research and better mental health care."
    B. The following are just some of the services provided by AMI of Dane County:
       1. Support Groups
          a. Parent Support Group—for persons with a son or daughter who suffers from a serious mental illness.
          b. Sibling and Adult Children Support Group—for persons with a brother, sister, or parent with mental illness.
          c. Spouse Support Group—for persons whose spouse has a severe mental illness.

2. Program Meetings—monthly meetings that have an informational program as the focus.
3. Library—the AMI library has numerous books, articles, videotapes and audiotapes for family members to borrow.

II. Suggested Reading
A. Informational books about the major mental illnesses
  1. Schizophrenia
     Torrey, E. F. (1988). *Surviving schizophrenia: A family manual, Revised ed.* New York: Harper & Row
  2. Bipolar Disorder (Manic Depression)
     Fieve, R. (1975). *Mood swings: The third revolution in psychiatry.* New York: Bantam.
  3. Unipolar Depression (Major/Severe Depression)
     Griest, J., & Jefferson, J. W. (1984). *Depression and its treatment: Help for the nation's No. 1 mental health problem.* Washington, DC: American Psychiatric Association Press.

     Styron, W. (1992). *Darkness visible: A memoir of madness.* New York: First Vintage/Random House.

B. Current information
   The Information Centers of the University of Wisconsin-Madison, Department of Psychiatry, 600 Highland Avenue, Madison, WI 53792; phone (608) 263-6171.

   You can call or write for the most current information on unipolar depression, bipolar disorder, obsessive-compulsive disorder, and child psychopharmacology.

C. Books written for family members of people with SMI
   Backlar, P. (1994). *The family face of schizophrenia.* New York: J. P. Tarcher/Putnam.

   Berger, D., & Berger, L. (1991). *We heard the angels of madness.* New York: Quill/William Morrow.

   Bernheim, K., Lewine, R., & Beale, C. (1982). *The caring family: Living with chronic mental illness.* New York: Random House.

Dearth, N., Labenski, R., Mott, E., & Pellegrini, L. (1986). *Families helping families: Living with schizophrenia.* New York: Norton.

Deveson, A. (1991). *Tell me I'm here.* New York: Penguin.

Dickens, R. M., & Marsh, D. T. (Eds.) (1994). *Anguished voices: Siblings and adult children of persons with psychiatric disabilities, Vol. 2,* No. 1. Psychiatric Rehabilitation and Community Support monograph. Boston: Boston University.

Moorman, M. (1992). *My sister's keeper.* New York: Norton.

Swados, E. (1991). *The four of us.* New York: Farrar, Strauss & Giroux.

Tallard Johnson, J. (1988). *Hidden victims: An eight-stage healing process for families and friends of the mentally ill.* New York: Doubleday.

Tallard Johnson, J. (1989). *Understanding mental illness: For teens who care about someone with mental illness.* Minneapolis: Lerner Publications.

Wasow, M. (1982). *Coping with schizophrenia: A survival manual for parents, relatives, and friends.* Palo Alto: Science and Behavior Books.

Index

About the Author

Mona Wasow is a clinical professor of social work at the University of Wisconsin, Madison, where she chairs the concentration in severe mental illnesses. Over her lifespan, she has published numerous papers and done workshops in the areas of family planning, human sexuality, aging, and severe mental illness.

When not teaching and writing, her joys revolve around the three grown children, her grandchildren, travel, hiking, and playing the piano and autoharp. Her next ambition is to get to Antarctica to watch penguins squabbling over rocks.

About the Artist

Elinor Randall studied drawing with Marshal Glasier in Madison, Wisconsin. This is where she met Mona Wasow and where she began with her the endless discussion of why and what humans do and think and feel. She lives in Plainfield, Vermont on an old farm, transposing words into lines and washes.